DATE DUE

NIKITA KHRUSHCHEV

NIKITA KHRUSHCHEV

Martin Ebon

1986
CHELSEA HOUSE PUBLISHERS
NEW YORK
NEW HAVEN   PHILADELPHIA

SENIOR EDITOR: William P. Hansen
ASSOCIATE EDITORS: John Haney
Richard Mandell
Marian W. Taylor
EDITORIAL COORDINATOR: Karyn Gullen Browne
EDITORIAL STAFF: Pierre Hauser
Perry Scott King
Alma Rodriguez-Sokol
John Selfridge
Bert Yaeger
ART DIRECTOR: Susan Lusk
LAYOUT: Irene Friedman
ART ASSISTANTS: Noreen Lamb
Carol McDougall
Tenaz Mehta
Victoria Tomaselli
COVER DESIGN: Mike Stromberg
PICTURE RESEARCH: Matthew Miller
Julie Nichols

Copyright © 1986 by Chelsea House Publishers, a division of Chelsea
House Educational Communications, Inc. All rights reserved. Printed and
bound in the United States of America.

First Printing

Library of Congress Cataloging in Publication Data

Ebon, Martin. NIKITA KHRUSHCHEV

(World leaders past & present)
Bibliography: p.
Includes index
  1. Khrushchev, Nikita Sergeevich, 1894–1971—
Juvenile literature.   2. Heads of state—Soviet
Union—Biography—Juvenile literature.
I. Title. II. Series.
DK275.K5E26   1986   947.085'2'0924 [B] [92]   85—19058
ISBN 0-87754-562-6

Chelsea House Publishers
Harold Steinberg, Chairman & Publisher
Susan Lusk, Vice President
A Division of Chelsea House Educational Communications, Inc.

133 Christopher Street, New York, NY 10014

345 Whitney Avenue, New Haven, CT 06510

5014 West Chester Pike, Edgemont, PA 19208

Photos courtesy of AP/Wide World Photos, Art Resource, The Bettmann
Archive, The German Information Center, Library of Congress and UPI/
Bettmann Newsphotos

Contents

CHELSEA HOUSE PUBLISHERS

WORLD LEADERS PAST & PRESENT

ADENAUER
ALEXANDER THE GREAT
MARK ANTONY
KING ARTHUR
KEMAL ATATÜRK
CLEMENT ATTLEE
BEGIN
BEN GURION
BISMARCK
LEON BLUM
BOLÍVAR
CESARE BORGIA
BRANDT
BREZHNEV
CAESAR
CALVIN
CASTRO
CATHERINE THE GREAT
CHARLEMAGNE
CHIANG KAI-SHEK
CHOU EN-LAI
CHURCHILL
CLEMENCEAU
CLEOPATRA
CORTEZ
CROMWELL
DANTON
DE GAULLE
DE VALERA
DISRAELI
EISENHOWER
ELEANOR OF AQUITAINE
QUEEN ELIZABETH I
FERDINAND AND ISABELLA

FRANCO
FREDERICK THE GREAT
INDIRA GANDHI
GANDHI
GARIBALDI
GENGHIS KHAN
GLADSTONE
HAMMARSKJÖLD
HENRY VIII
HENRY OF NAVARRE
HINDENBURG
HITLER
HO CHI MINH
KING HUSSEIN
IVAN THE TERRIBLE
ANDREW JACKSON
JEFFERSON
JOAN OF ARC
POPE JOHN XXIII
LYNDON JOHNSON
BENITO JUÁREZ
JFK
KENYATTA
KHOMEINI
KHRUSHCHEV
MARTIN LUTHER KING
KISSINGER
LENIN
LINCOLN
LLOYD GEORGE
LOUIS XIV
LUTHER
JUDAS MACCABEUS

MAO
MARY, QUEEN OF SCOTS
GOLDA MEIR
METTERNICH
MUSSOLINI
NAPOLEON
NASSER
NEHRU
NERO
NICHOLAS II
NIXON
NKRUMAH
PERICLES
PERÓN
QADDAFI
ROBESPIERRE
ELEANOR ROOSEVELT
FDR
THEODORE ROOSEVELT
SADAT
SUN YAT-SEN
STALIN
TAMERLAINE
THATCHER
TITO
TROTSKY
TRUDEAU
TRUMAN
QUEEN VICTORIA
WASHINGTON
CHAIM WEIZMANN
WOODROW WILSON
XERXES

Further titles in preparation

ON LEADERSHIP

Arthur M. Schlesinger, jr.

LEADERSHIP, it may be said, is really what makes the world go round. Love no doubt smooths the passage; but love is a private transaction between consenting adults. Leadership is a public transaction with history. The idea of leadership affirms the capacity of individuals to move, inspire and mobilize masses of people so that they act together in pursuit of an end. Sometimes leadership serves good purposes, sometimes bad; but whether the end is benign or evil, great leaders are those men and women who leave their personal stamp on history.

Now, the very concept of leadership implies the proposition that individuals can make a difference. This proposition has never been universally accepted. From classical times to the present day, eminent thinkers have regarded individuals as no more than the agents and pawns of larger forces, whether the gods and goddesses of the ancient world or, in the modern era, race, class, nation, the dialectic, the will of the people, the spirit of the times, history itself. Against such forces, the individual dwindles into insignificance.

So contends the thesis of historical determinism. Tolstoy's great novel *War and Peace* offers a famous statement of the case. Why, Tolstoy asked, did millions of men in the Napoleonic wars, denying their human feelings and their common sense, move back and forth across Europe slaughtering their fellows? "The war," Tolstoy answered, "was bound to happen simply because it was bound to happen." All prior history predetermined it. As for leaders, they, Tolstoy said, "are but the labels that serve to give a name to an end and, like labels, they have the least possible connection with the event." The greater the leader, "the more conspicuous the inevitability and the predestination of every act he commits." The leader, said Tolstoy, is "the slave of history."

Determinism takes many forms. Marxism is the determinism of class, Nazism the determinism of race. But the idea of men and women as the slaves of history runs athwart the deepest human instincts. Rigid determinism abolishes the idea of human freedom—the assumption of free choice that underlies every move we make, every word we speak, every thought we think. It abolishes the idea of human responsibility, since it is manifestly unfair to reward or punish people for actions that are by definition beyond their control. No one can live consistently by any deterministic creed. The Marxist states prove this themselves by their extreme susceptibility to the cult of leadership.

More than that, history refutes the idea that individuals make no difference. In December 1931 a British politician crossing Park Avenue in New York City between 76th and 77th Streets around ten-thirty at night looked in the wrong direction and was knocked down by an automobile—a moment, he later recalled, of a man aghast, a world aglare: "I do not understand why I was not broken like an eggshell or squashed like a gooseberry." Fourteen months later an American politician, sitting in an open car in Miami, Florida, was fired on by an assassin; the man beside him was hit. Those who believe that individuals make no difference to history might well ponder whether the next two decades would have been the same had Mario Contasini's car killed Winston Churchill in 1931 and Giuseppe Zangara's bullet killed Franklin Roosevelt in 1933. Suppose, in addition, that Adolf Hitler had been killed in the street fighting during the Munich *Putsch* of 1923 and that Lenin had died of typhus during the First World War. What would the 20th century be like now?

For better or for worse, individuals do make a difference. "The notion that a people can run itself and its affairs anonymously," wrote the philosopher William James, "is now well known to be the silliest of absurdities. Mankind does nothing save through initiatives on the part of inventors, great or small, and imitation by the rest of us—these are the sole factors in human progress. Individuals of genius show the way, and set the patterns, which common people then adopt and follow."

Leadership, James suggests, means leadership in thought as well as in action. In the long run, leaders in thought may well make the greater difference to the world. But, as Woodrow Wilson once said, "Those only are leaders of men, in the general eye, who lead in action. . . . It is at their hands that new thought gets its translation into the crude language of deeds." Leaders in thought often invent in solitude and obscurity, leaving to later generations the tasks of imitation. Leaders in action—the leaders portrayed in this series— have to be effective in their own time.

And they cannot be effective by themselves. They must act in response to the rhythms of their age. Their genius must be adapted, in a phrase of William James's, "to the receptivities of the moment." Leaders are useless without followers. "There goes the mob," said the French politician hearing a clamor in the streets. "I am their leader. I must follow them." Great leaders turn the inchoate emotions of the mob to purposes of their own. They seize on the opportunities of their time, the hopes, fears, frustrations, crises, potentialities.

They succeed when events have prepared the way for them, when the community is waiting to be aroused, when they can provide the clarifying and organizing ideas. Leadership ignites the circuit between the individual and the mass and thereby alters history.

It may alter history for better or for worse. Leaders have been responsible for the most extravagant follies and most monstrous crimes that have beset suffering humanity. They have also been vital in such gains as humanity has made in individual freedom, religious and racial tolerance, social justice and respect for human rights.

There is no sure way to tell in advance who is going to lead for good and who for evil. But a glance at the gallery of men and women in *World Leaders—Past and Present* suggests some useful tests.

One test is this: do leaders lead by force or by persuasion? By command or by consent? Through most of history leadership was exercised by the divine right of authority. The duty of followers was to defer and to obey. "Theirs not to reason why,/ Theirs but to do and die." On occasion, as with the so-called "enlightened despots" of the 18th century in Europe, absolutist leadership was animated by humane purposes. More often, absolutism nourished the passion for domination, land, gold and conquest and resulted in tyranny.

The great revolution of modern times has been the revolution of equality. The idea that all people should be equal in their legal condition has undermined the old structures of authority, hierarchy and deference. The revolution of equality has had two contrary effects on the nature of leadership. For equality, as Alexis de Tocqueville pointed out in his great study *Democracy in America*, might mean equality in servitude as well as equality in freedom.

"I know of only two methods of establishing equality in the political world," Tocqueville wrote. "Rights must be given to every citizen, or none at all to anyone . . . save one, who is the master of all." There was no middle ground "between the sovereignty of all and the absolute power of one man." In his astonishing prediction of 20th-century totalitarian dictatorship, Tocqueville explained how the revolution of equality could lead to the "*Führerprinzip*" and more terrible absolutism than the world had ever known.

But when rights are given to every citizen and the sovereignty of all is established, the problem of leadership takes a new form, becomes more exacting than ever before. It is easy to issue commands and enforce them by the rope and the stake, the concentration camp and the *gulag*. It is much harder to use argument and achievement to overcome opposition and win consent. The Founding Fathers of the United States understood the difficulty. They believed that history had given them the opportunity to decide, as

Alexander Hamilton wrote in the first Federalist Paper, whether men are indeed capable of basing government on "reflection and choice, or whether they are forever destined to depend . . . on accident and force."

Government by reflection and choice called for a new style of leadership and a new quality of followership. It required leaders to be responsive to popular concerns, and it required followers to be active and informed participants in the process. Democracy does not eliminate emotion from politics; sometimes it fosters demagoguery; but it is confident that, as the greatest of democratic leaders put it, you cannot fool all of the people all of the time. It measures leadership by results and retires those who overreach or falter or fail.

It is true that in the long run despots are measured by results too. But they can postpone the day of judgment, sometimes indefinitely, and in the meantime they can do infinite harm. It is also true that democracy is no guarantee of virtue and intelligence in government, for the voice of the people is not necessarily the voice of God. But democracy, by assuring the rights of opposition, offers built-in resistance to the evils inherent in absolutism. As the theologian Reinhold Niebuhr summed it up, "Man's capacity for justice makes democracy possible, but man's inclination to injustice makes democracy necessary."

A second test for leadership is the end for which power is sought. When leaders have as their goal the supremacy of a master race or the promotion of totalitarian revolution or the acquisition and exploitation of colonies or the protection of greed and privilege or the preservation of personal power, it is likely that their leadership will do little to advance the cause of humanity. When their goal is the abolition of slavery, the liberation of women, the enlargement of opportunity for the poor and powerless, the extension of equal rights to racial minorities, the defense of the freedoms of expression and opposition, it is likely that their leadership will increase the sum of human liberty and welfare.

Leaders have done great harm to the world. They have also conferred great benefits. You will find both sorts in this series. Even "good" leaders must be regarded with a certain wariness. Leaders are not demigods; they put on their trousers one leg after another just like ordinary mortals. No leader is infallible, and every leader needs to be reminded of this at regular intervals. Irreverence irritates leaders but is their salvation. Unquestioning submission corrupts leaders and demeans followers. Making a cult of a leader is always a mistake. Fortunately hero worship generates its own antidote. "Every hero," said Emerson, "becomes a bore at last."

The signal benefit the great leaders confer is to embolden the rest of us to live according to our own best selves, to be active, insistent, and resolute in affirming our own sense of things. For great leaders attest to the reality of human freedom against the supposed inevitabilities of history. And they attest to the wisdom and power that may lie within the most unlikely of us, which is why Abraham Lincoln remains the supreme example of great leadership. A great leader, said Emerson, exhibits new possibilities to all humanity. "We feed on genius. . . . Great men exist that there may be greater men."

Great leaders, in short, justify themselves by emancipating and empowering their followers. So humanity struggles to master its destiny, remembering with Alexis de Tocqueville: "It is true that around every man a fatal circle is traced beyond which he cannot pass; but within the wide verge of that circle he is powerful and free; as it is with man, so with communities."

—*New York*

1

Crisis in Cuba

Halfway through the 20th century, an unlikely statesman stepped onto the world stage. He was short, bald, paunchy, and wore baggy suits. He had little of the caution and self-restraint that powerful men usually display. His name was Nikita Khrushchev and for more than 10 years, from 1954 to 1964, he was the leader of the Soviet Union.

In 1962 Nikita Khrushchev flung a fearsome challenge at the United States and its president, John F. Kennedy. For 13 long days, the Soviet premier and the American president were locked in a confrontation that could have plunged the world into nuclear war.

The crisis began on October 16, 1962, when President Kennedy learned that for several months the Soviets had been installing powerful nuclear missiles on the Caribbean island of Cuba, which was situated only 90 miles from Florida. Once they had become operational, the missiles would pose a threat to large sections of the United States, including major cities on the East Coast. Photographs taken by American reconnaissance aircraft showed clearly that work on the missile sites was nearing completion.

Kennedy decided that he could not allow the missiles to remain in Cuba. But it did not seem likely

The Cuban missile crisis, which pitted the United States against the Soviet Union, marked history's first "eyeball-to-eyeball" nuclear confrontation. As the crisis escalated, the United States readied its massive arsenal of weapons, such as this *Titan* ICBM (intercontinental ballistic missile), shown rising from its underground silo in California.

Nikita S. Khrushchev (1894—1971) at the Soviet consulate in New York City in 1960. Both an outstanding statesman and a shrewd, sometimes ruthless politician, Khrushchev left a powerful imprint on his own nation, on world communism, and on world history.

Fidel Castro (left), Cuba's premier since 1959, embraces a new friend, Nikita Khrushchev, at the United Nations in 1960. Castro later said Khrushchev had congratulated himself for stationing missiles in Cuba, claiming that not even Stalin would have taken such a gamble.

that the Soviets would remove the missiles unless the president threatened to use force. If he did use force, however, there was the risk of triggering a nuclear war. It was a delicate and extremely dangerous situation.

Kennedy had met Khrushchev for the first time just a year earlier, in Vienna, the capital of Austria. This encounter had not succeeded in helping the two men establish a working relationship. The Soviet leader, 67 years old at the time and a veteran of many political battles, had found the young American president weak and inexperienced. Now he was challenging Kennedy and the United States directly. In the White House, Kennedy's staff tried to judge Khrushchev's motives. They had reason to believe that the quality of his leadership was coming under criticism from his colleagues in the Soviet government, and they wondered if Khrushchev's daring move in Cuba was an attempt to strengthen his position against his rivals.

Well before the missile crisis began, Kennedy had been growing concerned about the expanding Soviet influence in Cuba and the increased extent to which the island's head of state, Fidel Castro, was pursuing policies that the American government considered hostile to its interests. In January 1961 Kennedy's predecessor, President Dwight D. Eisenhower, had severed all diplomatic relations with Cuba because of that country's growing ties with the Soviet Union. Three months later Kennedy had authorized an invasion of the island by American-financed Cuban exiles intent on overthrowing Castro. However, the Cuban military crushed the ill-conceived assault with ease, causing the United States severe political embarrassment.

In 1959 former U.S. Navy pilot Alan Nye (left) was found guilty of plotting to assassinate Cuban Premier Fidel Castro (b. 1927) and deported from Cuba. The U.S. intelligence agencies over the years have concocted many seemingly impractical schemes to dispose of Castro, including lacing his cigars with toxins and using thallium salts to make his beard fall out.

On September 13, 1962, Kennedy said that if the "Communist buildup in Cuba were to endanger or interfere with our security in any way," or if Cuba ever became "an offensive military base of significant capacity for the Soviet Union," then the United States would do "whatever must be done to protect its own security and that of its allies." Kennedy repeated this warning to Soviet Foreign Minister Andrei A. Gromyko on October 18. Gromyko tried to assure the president that there was no need to worry, that the Soviet Union was merely concerned about Cuba's defenses.

By then, however, Kennedy already had proof to the contrary. Photographs taken by American U-2 spy planes flying over the Cuban town of San Cristobal had yielded incontrovertible evidence that the Soviets were installing intermediate- and medium-

Soviet Foreign Minister Andrei Gromyko (left; b. 1909) confers with John F. Kennedy (1917–1963) at the White House. Gromyko told the U.S. president that his nation had installed only short-range, surface-to-air missiles in Cuba. In reality, Khrushchev had sent dozens of long-range nuclear missiles, along with 22,000 Soviet troops and technicians.

range ballistic missiles. Kennedy knew Gromyko was lying, and he was furious at the Soviets' attempts to mislead him.

President Kennedy announced the crisis to the American public on Monday, October 22. Speaking on television and radio, he demanded the withdrawal of the missiles and declared that the U.S. Navy would blockade the island to prevent further Soviet supplies from reaching Cuba.

During the next week messages flew back and forth between Washington and Moscow. For the first three days after Kennedy's decision to blockade Cuba, Khrushchev's tone was belligerent. Then his messages became softer, almost pleading at times. Theodore Sorensen, a member of Kennedy's staff, observed that Khrushchev "seemed to be seeking a consensus among the top Kremlin rulers." (The

There is no need for the Soviet Union to site defensive weapons—weapons designed to administer retaliatory blows— in any other country (Cuba for instance). Our nuclear weapons are so devastating, and the rockets that would carry our warheads so powerful, that we do not need to search for suitable sites outside the Soviet Union.
—quoted from a Soviet government press statement issued by the state news agency, Tass, September 12, 1962

President Kennedy announces America's response to the installation of Soviet missiles in Cuba. He ordered U.S. Navy ships to encircle the island, U.S. Air Force planes to patrol the skies, and 12,000 Marines to prepare for invasion.

Displaying such messages as "Hands off Cuba" and "Shame on the USA," a Moscow crowd protests the U.S. blockade of Cuba during the 1962 missile crisis. Demonstrations also occurred in the United States, where Americans demanded an end to the Soviet presence in Cuba.

Kremlin is the headquarters of the Soviet government.) His contradictory behavior, ranging from hostile to conciliatory, did in fact seem to reflect the possibility that a power struggle was taking place within the Soviet leadership.

Moscow newspaper headlines during the crisis also alternated between violent attacks on America and pleas for world peace. On October 24 the official Communist party newspaper, *Pravda* (*Truth*), asserted: "The unleashed American aggressors must be stopped." On the following day the signals were mixed: "The aggressive designs of the American imperialists must be foiled. Peace on earth must be defended and strengthened!" On October 26 *Pravda* proclaimed: "Everything to prevent war." The following day the paper repeated Communist party slogans denouncing "imperialist warmongers" and calling for "lasting and indestructible peace." On the last day of the crisis *Pravda* merely stated: "We must defend and consolidate peace on earth."

The conflicting indications from Moscow undoubtedly reflected changes in Khrushchev's standing among his Kremlin colleagues. At first they had approved Khrushchev's bold gamble in Cuba. But when the crisis broke, Kremlin opinion was split over whether to stand fast or give in.

Kennedy's advisors also disagreed about whether they should take action immediately or wait for fur-

We must not tug at the ends of the rope in which you have tied the knot of war, because the harder we both pull, the tighter the knot will become. And a time may come when the knot is so tight that even he who tied it will not have the strength to undo it—and then the rope itself will have to be cut. Let us not simply slacken the rope; let us also take measures to undo the knot. We are ready for that.
—NIKITA KHRUSHCHEV
in a message to American
President John F. Kennedy,
October 26, 1962

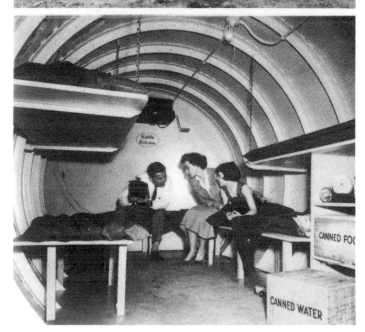

In the late 1950s and early 1960s an increasing number of Americans, worried about the possibility of nuclear war, built backyard bomb shelters and stocked them with emergency provisions. Understandably, the Cuban missile crisis did little to alleviate public anxiety.

A U.S. Marine sentry at Guantanamo Naval Base. Following the Spanish-American War in 1898, Cuba gave the United States permanent control of the base and the right to intervene in Cuba "to preserve order." The intervention agreement was revoked in 1934, but Guantanamo remained U.S. property.

ther developments. The longer the United States permitted Khrushchev to stall on his response to Kennedy's demand that the missiles be removed, the greater the chance that the missiles would be firmly in place, aimed directly at targets in the United States. Some officials on the president's staff wanted to bomb the missile bases; others argued for a full-scale invasion of Cuba. Kennedy, however, realized that it was important not to drive Khrushchev into a hopeless corner. He was determined to allow Khrushchev some room for maneuver so that the Soviet leader need not suffer a crippling blow to his prestige should he decide to remove the missiles.

Eighteen Soviet freighters were on their way to Cuba when Kennedy announced the blockade. The U.S. Navy tightened its control of all sea approaches to the island. At the same time, U.S. forces all over the world were coming to combat readiness. Soviet radar and satellites were undoubtedly tracking these preparations.

To the world's relief the Soviet ships turned back. Khrushchev had decided that he was playing for stakes that were too high. He had certainly misjudged the young American president, and his attempt to extend Soviet power into the Caribbean had failed. Under immense pressure at home, and with his credibility on the line, Khrushchev had the good sense to retreat. On October 28 he agreed to dismantle and remove the missiles in exchange for a U.S. pledge not to invade Cuba.

If Khrushchev had managed to keep the missiles in Cuba, the world scene might look very different today. Even if the missiles had never been used, they would have given the Russians a deadly bargaining chip, both in military confrontations and in arms negotiations. Michel Tatu, former Moscow correspondent of a Paris newspaper, discussed this point in his book *Power in the Kremlin*: "The missiles,

A November 4, 1962, U.S. Defense Department photograph revealed homeward-bound Soviet missiles, ready to be loaded onto waiting Soviet freighters at the Cuban port of Mariel. The removal of the missiles was claimed as a diplomatic victory by both the United States and the Soviet Union.

MISSILE EQUIPMENT
MARIEL PORT FACILITY

like the rest of [Khrushchev's] arsenal, were meant to intimidate, not to be fired. They were to serve as a formidable instrument of pressure on the United States in future negotiations, and it is conceivable that Khrushchev himself meant to withdraw them some day—in exchange for substantial concessions, of course." Tatu and other experts believe that the world balance of power would have shifted in the Soviet Union's favor if Khrushchev had been successful.

Khrushchev's failure was a serious blow to his power and influence within the Soviet leadership. He did his best to shift the blame onto the United States and to portray himself as a great peacemaker for having removed the missiles. He pointed out that the United States had nuclear missiles in Turkey, not far from the Soviet border. He also claimed that the United States had been planning another invasion of Cuba. Khrushchev's effort to rewrite history was demonstrated in a speech he made on December 12, 1962. "On the morning of October 27," he said, "we received, from our Cuban comrades and from other sources, definite information that [a U.S. invasion] would take place within two or three days. The telegrams we received displayed extreme alarm, which was well founded. Immediate action was required to prevent an attack on Cuba and to preserve peace. A message was addressed to the president of the United States suggesting a decision that would naturally be acceptable."

Khrushchev went on to say, "We declared that if the United States pledged itself not to invade Cuba and also prevented an aggression against Cuba by its allies, the Soviet Union was prepared to withdraw from Cuba the armaments that the United States regarded as offensive."

Khrushchev's speech actually put the cart before the horse. The Cuban crisis began not with an American threat to invade the island, but with the deployment of Soviet missiles on Cuba. And the crisis did not end because Khrushchev was a great peacemaker, but because he was forced to retreat from an ill-considered and provocative course of action.

> *The United States is demanding that military equipment that Cuba needs for the purposes of self-defense should be removed from Cuban territory—a requirement that, naturally, no state that values its independence can meet.*
> —quoted from a statement issued by the Soviet government on October 23, 1962, at the height of the Cuban Missile Crisis

> *Peaceful coexistence implies complete renunciation of war as the means of settling questions at issue, as well as noninterference in the internal affairs of other countries.*
> —NIKITA KHRUSHCHEV speaking in April 1958

Their faces reflecting relief, Muscovites learn from the official newspaper *Pravda* (*Truth*) that Khrushchev had agreed to withdraw Soviet missiles from Cuba. Millions of people throughout the world breathed a sigh of relief when the missile crisis was concluded peacefully.

23

2

Stalin's Ghost

Nikita Khrushchev's life and career were largely influenced by the Soviet leader who preceded him— Joseph Stalin. Stalin, a ruthless dictator, had ruled for almost a quarter of a century, from 1929 to 1953. While he was alive, Stalin inspired awe, slavish admiration, and fear.

When Khrushchev came to power following Stalin's death in 1953, he was almost 60 years old. Though he was clearly the most powerful man in the Soviet Union, he was not the president or premier. He held the title of first secretary of the Communist party of the Union of Soviet Socialist Republics (U.S.S.R.), or Soviet Union.

The Communist party is the Soviet Union's only political party and its most important organization. The official government of the U.S.S.R. consists of a president, a premier, a legislative body called the Supreme Soviet, and a Supreme Court, but the real power lies with the Communist party. The man who rules the party rules the country. Sometimes the party leader is also the premier. For example, Stalin held both titles; in 1958 Khrushchev became premier as well as party secretary.

Lenin holds the rapt attention of soldiers in Moscow in 1919. A committed Marxist since the age of 19, Lenin was an eloquent speaker and phrase-maker. "So long as the state exists," he said, "there is no freedom. When freedom exists, there will be no state."

Vladimir Ilich Lenin (left; 1870–1924), founding father of the Soviet state, at first regarded Joseph Stalin (right; 1879–1953) as a hard-working and loyal ally. By the time Lenin realized—in 1922—that Stalin was scheming to take power, he had been incapacitated by a stroke and was unable to stop him.

Known to his admirers as "The Pen," leading Russian revolutionary Leon Trotsky (1879–1940) was a brilliant writer. Among his many works were *The Defense of Terrorism* and *My Life*. Defeated by Stalin in a fight for government control, Trotsky was exiled in 1929. In 1940 an assassin, acting on Stalin's orders, put an ice ax through Trotsky's brain at his home in Mexico City.

Khrushchev inherited from Stalin the leadership of a government first established by Vladimir I. Lenin, leader of the Russian Revolution of 1917 and founder of the Soviet Union. This revolution, which abolished the rule of Russia's *tsars* (emperors), was carried out in the name of the workers and peasants. It sought to improve their living conditions and to give them the civil rights and political freedoms that the tsars had denied them. Lenin, however, began a process of centralizing power in the hands of the party and its leader which minimized the democratic character of the new government.

Lenin did not trust Stalin. Before he died in 1924, he tried to warn the party that Stalin was a brutal man who would not make a good leader. This warning, known as "Lenin's Testament," was suppressed by Stalin, who was determined to take Lenin's place. He immediately began to eliminate everyone who might threaten his rise to power.

His first victim was Leon Trotsky, one of Lenin's closest colleagues. Stalin drove Trotsky into exile in 1928 and had him murdered in 1940. In his drive to consolidate his power, Stalin turned on one party official after another, accusing them of treason, sabotage, and other alleged crimes against the Soviet people. Many were sentenced to death after trials that were a travesty of justice. This campaign of oppression grew to horrifying proportions during the 1930s. Millions of people were killed, and millions more were sent to prison camps.

During this period, Nikita Khrushchev was moving up through the ranks of the Soviet leadership. Like other ambitious Communist party members, he was full of praise for Stalin. Khrushchev and his colleagues believed—or pretended to believe—that Stalin was a great leader. However, Khrushchev was later to speak out about Stalin's cruelties and failures.

Soviet citizens grew accustomed to seeing images of Stalin almost everywhere. For decades, the man Khrushchev was later to call a "monster" was worshipfully known as the "Man of Steel" and the "Universal Genius."

In 1970, six years after Khrushchev had been forced from power, a book entitled *Khrushchev Remembers* was published in the West. It was not clear how the book had been put together and smuggled out of the Soviet Union, but experts agreed that it was an authentic memoir written or perhaps dictated by Khrushchev. In it Khrushchev described some of his experiences during the Stalin era.

Khrushchev noted that Lenin had considered Stalin "basically brutish and not above abusing power." Lenin had also come to believe that there was "unquestionably something sick about Stalin." Khrushchev said that people of his own generation remembered how the "glorification of Stalin grew and grew" until it became a form of mass worship. Propagandistic portraits and statues of Stalin were everywhere—in homes, offices, farm communes, factories, and railroad stations, on highways and in public squares.

Nadezhda Stalin (1902–1932) was a beautiful girl of 17 when she married Stalin. More than twice her age, he proved to be an abusive and often violent husband. Svetlana, the couple's daughter, later wrote that her mother's suicide "deprived [Stalin's] soul of the last vestiges of human warmth."

During his years as leader of the Soviet Union, Nikita Khrushchev revised the status of many of Stalin's victims. Some who had been killed were publicly honored; some who had been imprisoned were released. But, as Khrushchev pointed out, "Many more still await rehabilitation and the reasons for their deaths are still hidden."

Khrushchev found it impossible to put Stalin's ghost to rest; The memory of Stalin haunted him constantly throughout his years as the dictator's successor. Specifically, he could not reconcile the "Great Terror" of Stalin's rule with his own conduct during that period. The question, "What were you doing, Khrushchev, while Stalin was tyrannizing the country?" was one that he had to avoid. This was not a problem for Khrushchev alone. Much of the Kremlin leadership, as well as the Soviet public, had either been entirely convinced of Stalin's integ-

From the 1930s on, official gatherings of the Soviet high command almost always included Khrushchev. Here, reviewing a military parade on the 19th anniversary of the Russian Revolution of 1917, Khrushchev is second from the left. Stalin is third from the right; he is flanked by Vyacheslav M. Molotov (left; b. 1890) and Lazar M. Kaganovich (1893–c. 1964).

Moscow and other Soviet cities were studded with billboards during Stalin's first Five Year Plan, which began in 1929. "To secure greatness, build socialism," says the sign, which also displays impressive—but often fictitious—reports on the program's successes.

rity or had at least never considered questioning his policies. To confront Stalin's crimes was, to some degree, to confront their own guilt.

The Khrushchev memoirs pay tribute to Stalin's wife, Nadezhda Alliluyeva. Khrushchev first met her in 1929, while they were both attending Moscow's Industrial Academy. Nadezhda was a chemistry student specializing in artificial fibers, and was also a Communist party organizer. The memoirs state that she gave Stalin favorable reports about Khrushchev's political abilities.

"During the years that followed," Khrushchev adds, "I stayed alive while most of my contemporaries, my classmates at the Academy, lost their heads as enemies of the people. I often asked myself,

'How was I spared?' I think part of the answer is that Nadezhda's reports helped determine Stalin's attitude toward me. I call it my lottery ticket. I drew a lucky lottery ticket when it happened that Stalin observed my activities through Nadezhda. It was because of her that Stalin trusted me. In later years he sometimes attacked and insulted me; but right up until the last day of his life he liked me."

Nadezhda Stalin committed suicide on November 9, 1932. She was a disillusioned woman. At one point she had written a critical report about the forced collectivization of Soviet agriculture. This was one of Stalin's most disastrous projects.

In 1929 Stalin had launched the first Five Year Plan, a program intended to modernize Soviet agriculture. Having decided that the Soviet Union's

An immense bucket of molten ore dwarfs workers in a steel plant built under the first Five Year Plan. Although Stalin exaggerated the industrial progress achieved under the plan, it did culminate in the construction of many imposing factories, dams, and canals.

prosperous private farmers, called *kulaks* were not efficient enough, he tried to herd them all onto huge, state-run farms, or collectives, that would be more productive. The kulaks resisted, and many thousands were killed or sent to labor camps. Instead of increasing production, Stalin nearly wrecked Soviet agriculture.

It was rumored that Khrushchev prevented the publication of Nadezhda's report. He later said that he did not know at the time how much suffering and hardship Stalin's policies brought to the nation's countryside: "It was not until many years later that I realized the extent of the starvation and repression which accompanied collectivization as carried out under Stalin."

Khrushchev admitted that he was disturbed when Stalin blamed "local party members" for the human tragedy and economic dislocation caused by his agricultural policy. The collectivization drive

Hungry children are fed at a Soviet soup kitchen. Famine stalked the Soviet Union in the wake of Stalin's disastrous collectivization program. While its exact number of victims will probably never be known, some experts have estimated that 5 to 10 million peasants starved to death between 1928 and 1934.

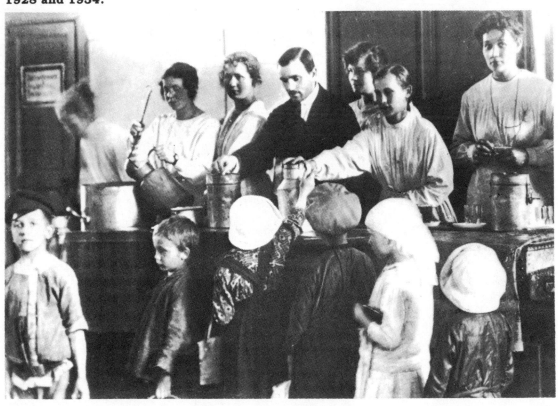

caused widespread destitution and mass deaths by starvation, conditions that historians in the West had long suspected and that Khrushchev's memoirs at last confirmed.

Khrushchev also substantiated what other visitors to Stalin's private villa had reported—that as Stalin grew older, he became increasingly paranoid. He made other people taste his food before he ate it since he distrusted even his closest associates. His villa came to resemble a fortress, with double walls and guard dogs everywhere, yet he surrounded himself with people at all times, and amused himself with long, exhausting parties. Once, after much consumption of vodka, Stalin ordered Khrushchev to perform a Ukrainian folk dance, the *gopak*. "He found the humiliation of others very amusing," Khrushchev recalled. But, as he later told a Kremlin colleague, "When Stalin says dance, a wise man dances."

A young Ukrainian woman takes part in a Soviet educational program. Only one out of every five Russians was literate before 1917, but in the wake of an intense literacy campaign that followed the revolution, more than 7 million illiterate adults were taught to read and write.

Before he grew suspicious of Molotov (center), Stalin (right) was frequently in the company of the old Bolshevik. Molotov outlived Stalin, but after he opposed Khrushchev in 1957, he fell from power.

The dictator's idea of entertainment was to subject his entourage to rambling monologues and seemingly endless sessions of privately screened movies. Films and dinners lasted far into the night. Khrushchev wrote: "These dinners were frightful. During the day I usually tried to take a nap, because there was always the risk that if you did not take a nap and Stalin invited you for dinner, you might get sleepy at the table; and those who got sleepy at Stalin's table could come to a bad end."

This was no exaggeration. Anyone who angered Stalin might be fired, imprisoned, or even killed. Stalin ruled by fear, and this fear infected his colleagues.

During his declining years Stalin suffered extreme loss of memory and became increasingly suspicious of his lieutenants. Having always ruled by terror and conspiracy, he had grown afraid that those around him were conspiring against him. Even two of his oldest comrades—Vyacheslav M. Molotov, who had long been Soviet foreign minister, and Anastas I. Mikoyan, a specialist in foreign trade—became targets of his paranoia.

Khrushchev wrote in his memoirs that Molotov

and Mikoyan had tried to "stay close to Stalin because they wanted to stay alive. For a while, whenever we went to the movies with Stalin, Molotov and Mikoyan showed up." But Stalin, noticing these tactics, had "raised an uproar" and shouted, "You think I do not see how you let Molotov and Mikoyan know when we are going to the movies? Stop telling them where I am! I will not tolerate it." Khrushchev was convinced that if Stalin had lived much longer, Molotov and Mikoyan "would have met a disastrous end."

One incident in particular mentioned by Khrushchev conjures up a powerful impression of Stalin's state of mind at the end of his life. Khrushchev and Mikoyan were visiting Stalin at his *dacha* (summer house) in Sukhumi, near the Black Sea. One day Stalin stepped out onto the porch. Seemingly unaware that his guests were within earshot, he said out loud, "I am finished. I trust no one, not even myself."

Moscow in the 1930s was a city of contrasts, its streets crowded with both threadbare peasants and well-dressed foreigners. It was also the scene of frantic construction activity, as Khrushchev and Kaganovich supervised the rapid erection of housing, public buildings, factories, schools, and the celebrated Metro subway.

3

Shepherd, Miner, Party Official

A working-class background is considered appropriate for Soviet officials because they rule in the name of the workers and peasants. Today most Soviet leaders are well-educated bureaucrats who have made long careers within the government or the Communist party. But Khrushchev could truly claim that he came from peasant stock.

Nikita Khrushchev was born in his grandfather's mud hut in the village of Kalinovka on April 17, 1894. Kalinovka is near the border between the Ukraine and what is now called the Russian Soviet Federated Socialist Republic (R.S.F.S.R.). (The Soviet Union is divided into 15 republics; the R.S.F.S.R. is the most important, and the Ukrainian Soviet Socialist Republic is next.)

"My grandfather was a serf," he said, "the property of a landlord who could sell him if he wished, or trade him for a hunting dog." The system of serfdom, similar to slavery, was part of Russia's economy for centuries, until Tsar Alexander II abolished it in 1861. Khrushchev said his father was "a farmer in the summer and a coal miner during the winter."

This photograph, taken by a British chemist working in Russia in 1912, offers a rare personal glimpse of a future Soviet leader. When the Briton, who had organized a soccer team, took his players to Moscow, they met a group of Russian amateurs that included an 18-year-old soccer enthusiast named Nikita Khrushchev (center).

Young Russian metalworkers ply their trade in an early 20th-century shop. The sharp contrast between the up-to-date methods used by foreign manufacturers and the primitive techniques that prevailed in Russia made a deep and lasting impression on the young Khrushchev.

The Khrushchev residence in the industrial community of Yuzovka (later Stalino and now Donetsk), where the family moved in 1908.

In 1908 Nikita's father decided to abandon farming altogether and moved the family to Yuzovka, a small industrial settlement in the Donbas region of the Ukraine, where he would work as a coal miner. He secured employment for his son at Yuzovka's Bosse factory, which was owned by a German company. There, Khrushchev quickly learned the skills of a fitter and mechanic. It was in the Bosse plant, according to Lazar Pistrak, in his biography of Khrushchev, *The Grand Tactician*, that "young Khrushchev for the first time saw East meeting West—the contrast between Western technological know-how and civilization and Eastern technical backwardness and primitive life." Khrushchev's later eagerness to have his country catch up with and overtake Western production "was perhaps born in this atmosphere of sharp contrast."

In 1914 the long-standing tensions between Europe's major powers (France, Germany, Austria-Hungary, Great Britain, and Russia) finally led to massive military conflict. World War I had begun, and Russia, which was allied with Britain and France, suffered a string of crushing defeats at the hands of the vastly more sophisticated and technologically advanced German army. Because his job was considered vital to the war effort, Khrushchev was not drafted into the army to fight the Germans. He continued to work as a fitter and became increasingly active in the revolutionary activity that was sweeping across Russia.

Even before the end of the 19th century, unrest had been growing among the Russian people. They wanted the kinds of political freedoms that were commonplace in western Europe, a greater share in their country's wealth, and a constitution. In the cities, the workers wanted better wages and working conditions. In the countryside, where most of the land was in the hands of a few rich property owners, the peasants wanted land and farms of their own.

Nicholas II, who had been tsar since 1894, was a harsh, unpopular, and inept ruler. Both his own credibility and that of his government had been greatly weakened in 1905 when Russia lost a war with Japan. At that time many people had revolted against the authorities, but the tsar's troops had managed to crush the rebellion. By the time of World War I there were many different groups working secretly to overthrow the tsar. The conspicuous inefficiency with which the government conducted the war eventually damaged its credibility to such an extent that the revolutionaries realized that an attempt to seize power would almost certainly succeed. In 1917 they staged a revolution. As they defended its gains during the next three years, thousands of aristocrats—including Nicholas and his entire family—were killed.

The Russian revolutionaries had all agreed that the tsar and his government had to go, but they could not agree on whom or what to put in their

I worked at a factory owned by Germans, at pits owned by Frenchmen, and at a chemical plant owned by Belgians. There I discovered something about capitalists. They are all alike, whatever their nationality. All they wanted from me was the most work for the least money that would keep me alive.
—NIKITA KHRUSHCHEV speaking in 1964 to British journalists concerning his early working life in tsarist Russia

Tsar Nicholas II (1868–1918) and Tsarina Alexandra (1872–1918) in 1904. When Nicholas abdicated in 1917, he and Alexandra, along with their five children, were arrested and imprisoned in the mountain town of Ekaterinburg. On the night of July 16, 1918, the royal family was ordered to a cellar and shot dead.

place. Some wanted to have a democratically elected government. Others wanted a communist system (a social order within which working people would no longer be exploited by the wealthy few) but thought that it would come naturally after a period of transition under a democratic government. The most radical group wanted to proceed to communism immediately, by force if necessary. This group, known as the Bolsheviks, was led by Vladimir Lenin.

A period of confusion and instability followed the overthrow of the tsarist regime. In 1918 Russia was torn by civil war between Lenin's supporters and those of the deposed tsar. The counterrevolutionary forces were joined by groups that had opposed the tsar but that also disagreed with Lenin. The anti-Bolshevik armies were aided by thousands of troops sent by Russia's former World War I allies, including Britain, France, and the United States. By 1920, however, the Bolshevik armies had triumphed and the revolutionary government was firmly in control.

By this time Khrushchev had taken part in various revolutionary activities. In his native village of Kalinovka (to which he had returned in 1917) he served as chairman of a committee of peasants who had seized property from the big landowners and divided it up among themselves.

In 1918 Khrushchev joined Lenin's Bolsheviks and fought on the side of the Red Army—the communist government's armed forces—in the civil war. "By the time the civil war was over in 1920," writes British historian Edward Crankshaw in *Khrushchev: A Career*, "he had in fact started to emerge as a useful and loyal figure, but still not a politician."

Khrushchev returned to the factory town of Yuzovka after the civil war. He was now a member of

A Russian artillery brigade straggles through the mountainous Manchurian countryside during the Russo-Japanese War in 1904. Russia, which had entered the war supremely confident of victory, suffered catastrophic military losses. The humiliating disaster added fuel to the fires of revolution already burning throughout Russia.

the ruling Communist party, and he had been appointed assistant manager of a coal mine that had been taken over by the workers. He had the difficult task of keeping up production under the disorganized conditions that followed the revolution and the civil war. In 1921 Khrushchev began attending the Donets Mining Technical School. About this time his wife, whom he had married in 1915, died, leaving him with two small children to look after.

Khrushchev quickly proved to be a talented organizer and administrator. However, the fact that he had left school at age 14 and had little formal education was an obstacle to his career. As a member of a party whose supporters were expected to be familiar with the writings of Karl Marx, the 19th-century German social and political philosopher whose ideas formed the basis of communism, he found himself at a serious disadvantage. Lenin and many other Bolsheviks were intellectuals who had studied Marx's theories deeply and used them as a guide to action. So Khrushchev began studying. By 1923 he was secretary of the school's Communist party organization and had acquired a basic understanding of Marxist thought. However, he would always retain a good deal of contempt for communists who concentrated exclusively on theory, and he never ceased to emphasize the importance of common sense and decisive action.

January 24, 1924, marked an important date in Soviet history—the day of Lenin's death. In the struggle for power that followed, Joseph Stalin gradually eliminated all competition and became dictator of the Soviet Union.

In 1925 one of Stalin's officials appointed Khrushchev Communist party secretary of the Yuzovka region, a territory about the size of Rhode Island. With him went Nina Petrovna Kukharchuk, whom he had married in 1923, and the children of his first marriage, Yulia and Leonid. With his second wife Khrushchev had two daughters, Rada and Yelena, and one son, Sergei.

Stalin spent the next 15 years tightening his control. As the process continued, his methods became increasingly brutal. He imprisoned or killed many

Everything depends on coal. How can the factories produce boots and shirts if they do not have coal? All you demand you must get with your hands. No manna from the sky is going to come down to you. So swing your picks with all your might.
—NIKITA KHRUSHCHEV
addressing Soviet miners
in 1921

Whip-wielding tsarist policemen slash at demonstrators on "Bloody Sunday"—January 22, 1905. Hundreds of striking workers were killed or wounded as they marched peacefully through St. Petersburg with a list of grievances for the tsar. Public outrage over the massacre severely damaged the credibility of the monarchy.

thousands of real or suspected enemies. Fear spread throughout the ranks of the Communist party and the Red Army.

Meanwhile, Khrushchev's career advanced steadily. He was helped by Lazar Kaganovich, who became general secretary of the central committee of the Ukrainian Communist party in 1925. That December, when the Fourteenth Congress of the All-Union Communist party—a meeting of party representatives from all the republics of the Soviet Union— took place in Moscow, Khrushchev was among the delegates.

In the speeches he made at party congresses during this period Khrushchev displayed his aggressive nature. In Crankshaw's opinion, Khrushchev became a "pacemaker" for Stalin and was "already committed by conviction to the development of authoritarian rule, which was to be the distinguishing feature of Stalin's career."

In 1929, after serving as an official in the Ukrainian city of Kiev for a year, Khrushchev went to work for Kaganovich in Moscow. Stalin had named Kaganovich secretary of the central committee of the

Women march in support of the revolution in 1917. The new Soviet government outlawed legal discrimination between the sexes; men and women now had equal privileges and obligations, including the right to vote and to sue for divorce.

"White" (Russian anti-Bolshevik) soldiers guard the bodies of slain "Red" (Bolshevik) troops in 1919. Although the tsar was gone and the nation had pulled out of World War I, Russia's death toll continued to mount as civil war raged between 1918 and 1921.

the All-Union Communist party, a major and powerful position. Both Khrushchev and his boss supported Stalin's efforts to suppress all activities within the Communist party that might challenge Stalin's one-man rule.

Khrushchev was both an observer of and a participant in Joseph Stalin's tyranny for about a quarter of a century. In his biography Pistrak concludes that Khrushchev "was not so much a blind follower of Stalin as a promoter of conditions necessary for the development of Stalin's dictatorial control."

In Moscow, in 1929, Khrushchev's first position was that of chief of the party cell at the Industrial Academy. (At the local level the Communist party is divided into small groups called "cells.") It was there that he met Stalin's wife, Nadezhda. His career within the Moscow party organization moved swiftly. By 1931 he was secretary of one of the city's

Expelled from Germany after his 1848 publication of *The Communist Manifesto*, Karl Marx (1818–1883) went to England. There, he wrote his masterpiece, *Das Kapital*. An analysis of the economics of capitalism, it became the bible of the Russian revolutionary movement.

party districts. He advanced to the post of first secretary of the Moscow party committee in 1935, and four years later he was a member of the politburo, the party's inner circle and its most powerful decision-making body.

Khrushchev's first years in Moscow coincided with the severe farm crisis that was triggered by Stalin's forced collectivization of agriculture. A few statistics prove the disastrous nature of Stalin's program. In 1929, Khrushchev's first year in the Soviet capital, the country had 34 million horses, 70 million head of cattle, and 130 million sheep and goats. Five years later, after starving farmers had been forced to eat their livestock, there were only 15 million horses, 30 million head of cattle, and a mere 36 million sheep and goats. Famine, starvation, illness, and death were widespread. Khrushchev said in his memoirs that he did not know about these terrible conditions while he was in Moscow.

Although Khrushchev later tried to play down his role in Stalin's regime, he in fact was deeply involved. According to Crankshaw, "The period of his rise, swift, uninterrupted, from a provincial agitator to one of Stalin's closest colleagues, coincided precisely with the ten years of Stalinism at its worst. This man, who was later to become one of the world's senior and in some ways most far-seeing and beneficent statesmen, achieved his eminence at a time when success could be obtained only by atrocious methods and over the dead or broken bodies of innumerable comrades."

An American member of the Allied Expeditionary Forces in Archangel, Russia, in 1919. By the end of 1918, 180,000 Allied soldiers—British, American, French, Japanese, Italian, and Greek—were on Soviet soil, supplying support—but not victory—to the 300,000 troops of the anti-Bolshevik Whites.

4

Moscow Years

The conflict between Khrushchev's natural humanity and the corruption which bit deeply into him during the years of his rise to the top was to be the great drama of the last ten years of his career.
—EDWARD CRANKSHAW
British journalist and historian

During the early 1930s Khrushchev assisted Kaganovich in administering the city of Moscow. Together they carried out most of Stalin's plans for modernizing the Soviet capital. Khrushchev coaxed, bullied, flattered, and threatened the thousands of workers employed in the city's numerous and extremely ambitious building projects. Because of strict timetables, he sometimes ignored difficulties in his haste to realize short-term targets. He boasted when buildings, bridges, and roads were completed on schedule.

The most monumental achievement of the Kaganovich-Khrushchev partnership was the construction of the Metro, Moscow's glittering subway system. It is still the city's most impressive tourist attraction. Because Stalin had demanded that the subway be a showcase of dazzling luxury, the Metro's stations feature such unlikely touches as elegant tile designs and elaborate chandeliers. According to a current tourist guidebook, the subway contains more marble than "all the palaces of tsarist Russia during the fifty years preceding the Great October Socialist Revolution."

Khrushchev (second from left) and his boss, Lazar Kaganovich (in white cap) inspect progress in the Moscow Metro in 1934. Kaganovich was a powerful Soviet leader until 1957, when he was expelled from the Communist party for joining a group aiming to depose Khrushchev. His subsequent fate is unknown.

Stalin and Khrushchev in 1936. Known for his curtness, Stalin could be charming to those he considered useful. Khrushchev was such a man, and he warmed to his leader's friendship. "I was," he wrote, "literally spellbound by Stalin, by his attentiveness, his concern."

The breathtaking Metro, sparkling under the streets of Moscow, provided a stark contrast to the bleak existence led by most Soviet citizens during the 1930s. Crankshaw writes of the paradox inherent in the magnificent subway system thus: "It is impossible to tell what the Muscovites really thought about this splendor. Crammed together, two families to a room in hovels, cellars, and crumbling apartment blocks; ill shod, wretchedly clothed, undernourished, they swarmed and pushed and cursed their way into the magic trains which swept silently out of the darkness, came to rest in these stations of glittering splendor, and whisked the triumphant proletarians away to their miserable homes, to their bleak factories, or to queue for hours in front of barren shops for the simplest necessities of life—a box of matches, a needle and thread."

Khrushchev was later to denounce Stalin for wasting money on ornamental buildings, which he called architectural expressions of the dictator's vanity. But while he was in charge of transforming Moscow, Khrushchev did his best to get them built. In 1936, when workers complained that work goals were too high, Khrushchev made an angry speech to a group of construction foremen. "Under the influence of self-seekers," he raged, "who have wormed themselves into our construction sites, some workers have begun to think along the following lines: why do we not try to get our norms revised downwards? Pernicious and disorganizing aspirations of this kind must be severely put down." Anyone who protested the harsh working conditions was an "opportunistic whisperer" guilty of supporting "counterrevolutionary elements."

The Moscow building projects, particularly the Metro, proceeded in great haste, sometimes causing tunnels and buildings to collapse along the subway route; cave-ins and flooding resulted in many deaths and injuries. Volunteers, including communists from abroad, were employed on the projects. Later, political prisoners were also used as slave labor.

As work on the Metro went ahead at a breakneck pace, furious political activity was unfolding above ground. Stalin's policy of removing his opponents one by one underwent substantial revision following the assassination of Sergei Mironovich Kirov, the dictator's chief deputy in Leningrad, on December 1, 1934. Kirov, whom some historians consider to have been a potential rival of Stalin, was killed by a young local communist. It is likely, however, that Stalin himself ordered the murder. He may have wanted his Leningrad deputy killed because of his fear of Kirov's considerable prestige and abilities and because of his resentment of the fact that Kirov had recently been making speeches that contained a measure of criticism (albeit somewhat veiled) of Stalin's agricultural policy. The dictator then used Kirov's death as an excuse for mass "show" trials, imprisonments, and executions of vast numbers of presumed enemies, and often their families too. Many—perhaps most—victims of the infamous purges of the 1930s were entirely innocent of the crimes of which they were accused.

The completed Metro was unquestionably the most magnificent structure of its kind in the world. Khrushchev received his first decoration—the prestigious Order of Lenin—for his part in its construction.

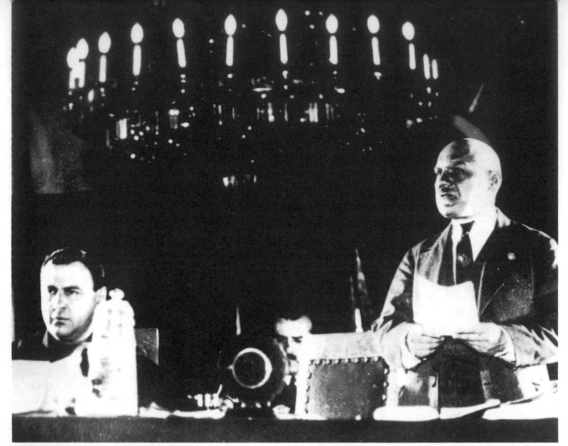

A prosecutor reads charges at a Moscow "show trial." These legal mockeries were carefully staged. As courtroom spectators shouted "Death to the wreckers!" at prescheduled intervals, thousands of workers would march in the streets chanting, "Death, death, death!" The sentences demanded by such "spontaneous" demonstrations were almost invariably carried out.

Khrushchev later agreed that "the circumstances surrounding Kirov's murder hide many things which are inexplicable and mysterious and demand a most careful examination." However, no such examination took place during the 10 years of Khrushchev's rule. His successors also preferred to keep silent about the Kirov murder and the years of the terrible Stalin purges.

Lazar Pistrak, in his biography of Khrushchev, writes that Khrushchev later tried to give the impression that he was "a powerless, insignificant party leader" both before and after the Kirov assassination. But, Pistrak reminds us again, Khrushchev "played a special role in creating the political and psychological climate needed to make Stalin's crimes possible."

On March 16, 1937, Khrushchev urged party officials to be alert to "wreckers and strangers," to watch out for enemies around them, and to avoid political "deafness or blindness." Earlier that year, he had endorsed the trumped-up charges against Stalin's supposed rivals at a mass meeting in Moscow's Red Square. *Pravda* said that the meeting had been attended by 200,000 people, and that Khrushchev had spoken as follows: "These murderers aimed at the heart and brain of our party. . . . By raising their villainous hands against Comrade Stalin they raised them against everything that is best in the possession of humanity. For Stalin is hope; he is expectation; he is the beacon that guides all progressive mankind. Stalin is our banner! Stalin is our will! Stalin is our victory!"

These praises of Stalin were typical of the time. Khrushchev was neither more nor less emphatic than others in championing Stalin's ruthless poli-

Let these enemies know that no matter how deep down they may sit in their burrows, we will uncover them, and scatter them to the four winds so that not even a trace will remain of these damned betrayers of the socialist motherland.
—NIKITA KHRUSHCHEV in a 1937 speech urging the Soviet people to ferret out what he called "concealed enemies"

The Soviet Union's four most powerful men carry the coffin of high Soviet official Sergei M. Kirov, who was assassinated in Leningrad in 1934. The pallbearers (left to right) are: Molotov; military chief Klementii E. Voroshilov (1881–1970); Stalin; and President Mikhail Kalinin (1875–1946). Kirov's death triggered the start of the Great Purge.

cies. Opportunism and fear were probably among Khrushchev's motives. He had succeeded under Stalin; if he did not enthusiastically support the dictator, he might join the countless millions who had perished in the prisons and labor camps.

According to Pistrak, Khrushchev "exposed" the "enemies of the people"—a term Stalin frequently used—and urged others to do likewise. So effective was Khrushchev in this particular role that Stalin selected him to complete the purges in the Ukraine, which at the time had a population of some 40 million. Khrushchev returned to his home territory armed with vast authority and Stalin's orders to eliminate all suspects. To justify such purges, Stalin and Khrushchev labeled their victims "Trotskyites," "fascists," or "spies." Of vital importance to the whole Soviet Union was the Ukraine's capacity to produce vast amounts of grain, but production deteriorated because of Stalin's excessively ambitious collectivization program. Between 1929 and 1934

A 1939 photomontage shows an eerie card game between German Foreign Minister Joachim von Ribbentrop (left; 1893–1946) and Stalin. The composite picture was a satirical comment on the Nazi-Soviet nonaggression treaty signed on August 23, 1939. Confident of Stalin's support, Nazi leader Adolf Hitler (1889–1945) invaded Poland a week later. World War II had begun.

the Ukraine had lost 50% of its horses, 40% of its cattle, 50% of its pigs, and 75% of its sheep and goats. Another important factor was the territory's industrial output, amounting to 50% of the Soviet Union's coal production, more than 50% of its pig iron, and 35% of its steel.

Among the many people selected for Khrushchev's particular attention in the Ukraine were the members of the nationalist movement, which consisted of a large number of peasants bitterly resentful of Moscow's iron rule. They hated collective farming and many of them slaughtered their livestock, destroyed their tools, and burned their crops in protest. It was Khrushchev's job to ensure that the harsh decrees instituted by Stalin to combat the peasants' resistance yielded tangible results. Under the new rules, peasants who failed to cooperate with collectivization could be killed or deported.

Khrushchev traveled throughout the Ukrainian countryside. When he discovered how few cattle

"Operation Barbarossa," the Nazi code name for the conquest of the Soviet Union, began at dawn on June 22, 1941, when Hitler's armies broke through Soviet defenses and penetrated deep into Soviet territory. On the same day, Germany's *Luftwaffe* (air force) crippled much of the Soviet air force.

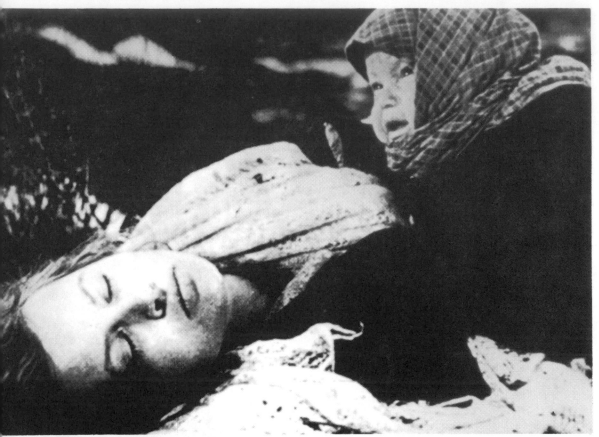

A Soviet child weeps over the body of her mother, killed during a Nazi assault on their village. Soviet war losses, both military and civilian, were appalling; 20 million people died, and one-quarter of the nation's property was destroyed.

were left on the farms, he would goad the administrators: "Ten cows to a collective farm? That's enough to make a chicken laugh!" At one meeting he upbraided a talkative official: "The milk yield of your cows will not increase, however much you wag your tongue!"

Acting on Stalin's behalf, Khrushchev effectively used terror and force to persuade the unwilling farmers of the Ukraine to participate in the new agricultural system. His methods were often brutal, but they worked. As one biographer, Mark Frankland, notes in his book *Khrushchev*: "By 1939, after two harvests under his care, Khrushchev was able to declare the grain problem solved." His administrative gifts, adds Frankland, "seemed to assure his future, now that the madness of the purges was over."

In August 1939 the German head of state, Adolf Hitler, and Soviet leader Joseph Stalin astonished the world by signing a nonaggression treaty. This pact between the Soviets and the violently anticommunist National Socialist government of Germany included a secret agreement that would divide Poland between the two states following the German invasion of that country, which commenced on September 1, 1939. The Soviets marched into Poland on September 17. With the incorporation of much of eastern Poland into the Ukraine, Khrushchev had to extend his administration to include another 9 million people, collectivize the farms, and superimpose a totally Soviet administration on a confused and resentful population. Soviet neutrality in the face of a conflict that saw France, Denmark,

Soviet defenders near Moscow in 1941. The Nazis were within 20 miles of the city by November 1941. In December, however, the Red Army counterattacked in full fury, killing 1 million Germans.

Lieutenant General Nikita Khrushchev (right) and General Nikolai Vatutin (1900–1944) discuss strategy before their recapture of the Ukrainian city of Kiev in 1943. The following year, Vatutin would die in a battle with Ukrainian nationalists and Khrushchev would be given the assignment of restoring order in the devastated region.

Norway, Luxembourg, Belgium, and the Netherlands defeated by Germany in 1940 and Britain fighting on alone thereafter came to an abrupt end in 1941. On June 22 Germany launched a massive surprise attack on the Soviet Union, and the Red Army came close to disintegrating. As Khrushchev later recalled, Stalin had consistently ignored warnings that a German invasion was imminent.

Frankland notes that, "up to the war there is no evidence that Khrushchev ever questioned" Stalin's judgment, but "this simple relationship was destroyed by the war and was never reestablished." Khrushchev remained in a secondary position within the Soviet leadership during the war. He first served as political and military chief of the Kiev Special Military District. However, German troops soon captured Kiev, and the Soviet armies retreated further eastward through the Ukrainian countryside.

Khrushchev accompanied the troops as they re-formed around the key city of Stalingrad. Here, the Soviet army stood its ground. The German forces at Stalingrad surrendered on January 31, 1943, and, from then on, the tables were turned. Soviet forces pushed Hitler's army back across all of eastern Europe and eventually entered Berlin, the German capital, early in 1945. In recognition of his wartime services to the Soviet Union, Khrushchev was promoted lieutenant general. As the war had raged on, Khrushchev had become increasingly aware of Stalin's weaknesses. He had also observed, at first hand, the devastation that modern war can cause. This combination of experiences was to explain much about Nikita Khrushchev's later conduct.

Stalingrad in 1942. Ferociously besieged by the German army, the Soviets defended the city with titanic determination, often engaging in hand-to-hand combat in streets and houses. By the end of 1942 the tide had turned; in January 1943, 91,000 Nazi soldiers surrendered. Stalingrad, however, had been reduced to rubble.

5

Kremlin Rivalries

The years following World War II demanded skill and energy on the part of Nikita Khrushchev. An estimated 20 million Soviet soldiers and civilians had died during the conflict, but Joseph Stalin was in no mood to pause for careful, step-by-step reconstruction. Instead, he returned to his prewar tactics, which demanded quick successes and economic sacrifices by the people.

The Ukraine, Khrushchev's special domain, had suffered immense devastation. Fields lay fallow. Forests had been denuded. The livestock population had been decimated. The Soviet government had ordered factories dismantled and had shipped equipment and farm animals eastward to save them from the advancing German armies. When the Germans retreated, they stripped the countryside of everything that was movable.

Stalin sent Khrushchev to rebuild the Ukraine, to rally the people to work for their own recovery. It was also part of his mission to crush the anti-Soviet guerrillas in the Ukrainian nationalist movement. Arriving in the Ukraine, Khrushchev was struck by the enormous scale of the damage caused by the

His political strength demonstrated by his position at Stalin's right hand, Georgi Malenkov (b. 1902) salutes a Moscow military parade in 1949. Personally selected by Stalin as his successor, Malenkov was eventually outmaneuvered by Khrushchev, stripped of all power in 1957, and expelled from the party in 1964.

The Kremlin, headquarters of the Soviet government, is a sprawling collection of onion-domed towers and stone structures that dominate Moscow, the Soviet capital. Originally built as a fortress, the Kremlin has been the hub of Russia's political life for centuries.

war and the defeated look of the ragged farm families just back from the woods and hills where they had hidden from the invaders. In his native village, Kalinovka, he grew angry at what he called "the indifference of the people." In a desperate attempt to inspire his audience, he made one of his typically fiery speeches. But he realized that to them he was "just like some sort of Martian, coming from who knows where and trying to make people believe in their own capabilities." He knew the villagers were waiting for him to leave and to "stop rubbing salt into their wounds."

Outside observers (including staff members of the United Nations Relief and Rehabilitation Administration, which was working in the Soviet Union at the time) spoke highly of Khrushchev's dedication

to his huge and difficult task. In contrast to desk-bound bureaucrats, he was always out in the fields, coal mines, and factories. Since the Ukraine was the breadbasket of the Soviet Union and also supplied much of the country's coal, its recovery was of vital importance. Stalin, aware of Khrushchev's competence, left his lieutenant alone to do what needed to be done.

During this postwar period of reconstruction, Stalin was experiencing a physical and mental decline that made him especially wary of those Soviet officials around him who displayed conspicuous ambition. He suspected them of eagerly anticipating his downfall. For what he considered to be his own protection, he played political power games with leading Soviet officials, pitting them against one another.

Away from the stifling atmosphere of Kremlin rivalries, Khrushchev was able to accomplish a great deal. And he did it with less coercion and arbitrary ruthlessness than was customary under Stalin's regime. In fact, his years in the Ukraine helped him to develop the freewheeling style that later became his trademark.

Khrushchev was not entirely safe from the power struggles that were going on in the Kremlin. Georgi Malenkov, Stalin's closest colleague, was determined to reduce Khrushchev's influence. For a period of six months in 1947 that coincided with a drought in the Ukraine, Malenkov appeared to have succeeded in pushing Khrushchev into the background. But Khrushchev bounced back. In 1949, when Stalin recalled him to Moscow, he arrived with the air of a man who had done well and was ready to go on to bigger and better things.

As it became increasingly obvious that Stalin was a sick man, his potential successors began to jockey for position. They were united only in their fear of the paranoid dictator as they battled for his favor in hopes of future power. Stalin, who wanted none of them to become too powerful, encouraged their infighting.

Stalin finally died on March 5, 1953. As indicated by his position at the dictator's funeral, Malenkov

> *It was Khrushchev's overwhelming vitality and drive which, coupled with his quickness and ingenuity, produced the impression that he was really going somewhere—and thus obscured the truth: namely that his mind was a politician's mind, the sort of mind found in all men who rise to power by persuasion and intrigue and who repose their power on the consent of the persuaded.*
> —EDWARD CRANKSHAW

**Lavrenti Beria, who had
commissioned thousands of
murders on Stalin's orders,
was hated and feared by the
dictator's heirs, Khrushchev
in particular. In his memoirs, published abroad in
1970, Khrushchev asserted
that Stalin himself was afraid
of Beria.**

emerged as the most prominent of the surviving
leaders. Malenkov headed the procession to the top
of the Lenin-Stalin tomb in Red Square. Behind him
was Lavrenti Beria, the shadowy, powerful chief of
the N.K.V.D., the Soviet Union's dreaded secret police. Then came Chinese Prime Minister Zhou Enlai,
Nikolai Bulganin, and Vyacheslav M. Molotov. Khrushchev and his former boss, Lazar Kaganovich,
brought up the rear.

Khrushchev did not stay at the end of the line for
long. Malenkov had quickly taken over the posts of
premier and first secretary of the Communist party.
Within two weeks of Stalin's death, however, he re-
linquished the second title, and Khrushchev became first among the party's five secretaries. For
most of the rest of 1953 Malenkov remained the
most prominent figure at public functions while
Khrushchev worked quietly behind the scenes.
Khrushchev strengthened his position by placing
trusted friends from his Ukrainian years in key
appointments.

In July 1953 Stalin's longtime henchman Beria
was quietly arrested. This much-feared man had
amassed enormous power as head of the secret police. For their own safety, his Kremlin colleagues
decided to eliminate him. After a secret trial later
that year, Beria was shot.

Meanwhile, the Soviet population was growing
rapidly, but, largely because of continued peasant
resistance to collectivization, food production was
not meeting the targets that the nation's planners
had set. In February 1954 Khrushchev told the ruling central committee in Moscow about his solution
to the severe agricultural crisis. The "Virgin Lands"
plan, which was one of his favorite projects, pro-
posed the plowing and planting of 32 million acres
of previously unexploited land in Siberia, the
Ukraine, and the central Asian republics—an area
equal to all the farmlands in Great Britain, France,
and Spain. The Virgin Lands program secured a
dramatic increase in Soviet grain production in
1954 and 1956, which greatly enhanced Khrushchev's prestige. Like other innovations in Soviet
agriculture, however, the program failed to live up

to the government's original expectations and had fallen drastically behind by 1960.

According to Crankshaw, 1954 was "Khrushchev's great year. Having got himself into the center of the limelight with the Virgin Lands campaign, he never moved out of it. Soon he was laying down the law, as first secretary, on every aspect of Soviet policy."

During the mid-1950s Khrushchev traveled throughout the Soviet Union and also attended Communist party meetings in Poland and Czechoslovakia, two of the several eastern European nations that had been firmly under Soviet control since shortly after the end of World War II. By now it had become apparent that he was beginning to overshadow Malenkov. In September 1954, accompanied by a delegation of experts, Khrushchev went to Beijing and arranged a crucial trade agreement with the communist government of the People's Republic of China. He had clearly become, in fact if not officially, top man in the Soviet Union.

On February 8, 1955, the 1,300 members of the Supreme Soviet, the Soviet Union's parliament, were told that Malenkov was resigning the post of premier. It was announced that he was being replaced "by another comrade of greater administrative experience." Khrushchev then nominated Nikolai Bulganin to succeed Malenkov.

You're a nice-looking lad, but how could you paint something like this? We should take down your pants and set you down in a clump of nettles until you understand your mistakes.
—NIKITA KHRUSHCHEV speaking to the Soviet painter Zheltovsky, while viewing a show of abstract art in Moscow

Millions of acres of rich earth were opened up under Khrushchev's "Virgin Lands" project. The Soviet Union's agricultural inefficiency was deeply frustrating to Khrushchev. "I look forward to the day," he said, "when a camel would be able to walk from Moscow to Vladivostok without being eaten by hungry peasants on the way."

Arriving in Beijing in 1954, Khrushchev is greeted by Chinese communist leader Mao Zedong (1893–1976). The warm relationship between the Soviet Union and China began to cool after Khrushchev's denunciation of Stalin in 1956; the ideological rift continued to widen and by 1963, the world's most powerful Marxist states were angrily censuring each other.

You all went to great schools, to famous universities—to Harvard, to Oxford, to the Sorbonne. I never had any proper schooling. I went about barefoot and in rags. When you were in the nursery I was herding cows for two kopecks. And yet here we are, and I can make rings around you all. Tell me gentlemen, Why?

—NIKITA KHRUSHCHEV speaking to a group of Western diplomats at a reception in Moscow

After decades of Stalin's autonomous rule, the Kremlin leadership was now supposed to be collective, the power being shared by the senior officials. But Khrushchev was determined to be first among equals—and a good deal more than that. He had engineered Malenkov's resignation because he knew that Malenkov was strong enough to be his rival. Bulganin, a white-bearded, mild-mannered man, was willing to sit by silently while Khrushchev held the center of the political stage.

When, in May 1955, the Kremlin sent a delegation to patch up the quarrel Stalin had picked with communist Yugoslavia's independent-minded leader, Marshal Josip Broz Tito, it was Khrushchev who made the trip and did most of the talking. He blamed Beria for the strain between the Soviet Union and Yugoslavia. He also told Tito confidentially that some of the negative aspects of the Stalin era would soon be made known to an audience far wider than that constituted by the late dictator's former colleagues.

Khrushchev and Bulganin attracted worldwide attention in visits to India, Burma, and Afghanistan in 1955. Next came a summit meeting in Geneva attended by heads of state and foreign ministers from the major Western and Eastern powers. Foreign Minister Vyacheslav Molotov was in attendance, but Khrushchev clearly dominated the Soviet delegation.

British Foreign Secretary Anthony Eden, writing in his memoirs, described the Soviet leader as "vigorous, downright, and stubborn, but prepared to laugh. A forceful personality, always ready to go over to the attack." Eden observed that while Bulganin was the official spokesman, "the authority of Khrushchev could always be felt when the two men were together." Molotov, the staunch Stalinist who was to be forced from power by Khrushchev in 1957, was clearly overshadowed at Geneva.

Nikolai A. Bulganin (center) and Khrushchev greet U.S. Secretary of State John Foster Dulles (1888–1959) in Geneva in 1955. Bulganin, a former defense minister, had just become premier with Khrushchev's blessing. Identified as a member of the "anti-party group," he was stripped of all power three years later.

6

Khrushchev's Secret Speech

On February 24, 1956, almost three years after Stalin's death, Khrushchev addressed the Twentieth Congress of the Communist party of the Soviet Union. His speech lasted for several hours, and when he had finished, a new era in Soviet history had begun. The 1,436 men and women who made up his audience were stunned. Khrushchev had delivered a 20,000-word condemnation of Joseph Stalin, the man they had followed as an all-wise leader, the head of state who had been described in millions of words as a kindly, progressive world figure. What only hours before had been a glorious page of history was suddenly a grisly record of terror and death.

Khrushchev told the truth as it had been gauged by Western historians and political commentators for many years. At some points he told even more than was publicly known abroad. Most of the time,

Alexander Solzhenitsyn (b. 1918) addresses a 1978 Harvard University commencement. The exiled Soviet author created a worldwide sensation with *One Day in the Life of Ivan Denisovich*, a 1962 novel detailing the horrors of Stalin's labor camps. Solzhenitsyn praised Khrushchev's 1956 liberation of millions of political prisoners; it was, he said, a "movement of the heart."

Khrushchev relaxes during a mid-1950s plane trip. Unlike Stalin, Khrushchev enjoyed traveling; he visited every part of the Soviet Union and many foreign countries. As one biographer put it, "He was not only his country's leader; he was her inspector-general."

however, he told only part of the truth. Since he and many others in his audience had supported Stalin throughout their careers, Khrushchev could not permit the whole truth about Stalin's deeds to become part of official Soviet history without aggravating suspicions about his own conduct during the period of Stalin's rule. Perhaps he felt that this candid speech could atone for much he had done, or felt he had been forced to do during those years. Regardless, as Bertram D. Wolfe says in his book *Khrushchev and Stalin's Ghost*, "The speech is perhaps the most important document ever to come from the Communist movement."

There had been hints earlier in the meeting that Joseph Stalin's regime would come under criticism. But even though other members of the Communist party leadership must have supported Khrushchev's daring move, the speech itself bore the stamp of his own forceful personality.

Khrushchev spoke of the dead leader's direct role in the arrest, imprisonment, and execution of innocent Soviet citizens. He described Stalin's paranoia: "Stalin was a very distrustful man, morbidly suspicious; we knew this from our work with him. He could look at a man and say: 'Why are you turning so much today and why do you avoid looking directly into my eyes?' The sickly suspicion created in him a general distrust even toward eminent party workers whom he had known for years. Everywhere and in everything he saw 'enemies,' 'two-facers' and 'spies.' Possessing unlimited power, he indulged in great willfulness and choked a person morally and physically."

Khrushchev presented an analysis of errors committed by Stalin during World War II, when the German armies had penetrated deeply into the Soviet Union. In August 1939 Stalin and Hitler had signed a treaty promising that their countries would not attack each other. But Hitler had soon unleashed his forces against Stalin just two years later, catching the Soviet leader completely by surprise. Khrushchev blamed Stalin for ignoring clear warnings that Hitler was preparing to invade.

"As you see," he told the delegates to the Twen-

Stalin originated the concept 'enemy of the people.' This term automatically rendered it unnecessary that the ideological errors of a man or men engaged in a controversy be proven; this term made possible the usage of the most cruel repression against anyone who in any way disagreed with Stalin, against those who were only suspected of hostile intent, against those who had bad reputations.
—NIKITA KHRUSHCHEV

tieth Congress, "everything was ignored: warnings of certain army commanders, declarations of deserters from the enemy army, and even the open hostility of the enemy. Is this an example of the alertness of the chief of the party and of the state at this particularly significant historical moment?"

Backed by a heroic statue of Lenin and the ranks of the central committee, Khrushchev presides over the opening session of the Twentieth Congress of the Soviet Communist party in February 1956. The hundreds of high Soviet officials present at the meeting were soon to be electrified by Khrushchev's denunciation of Stalin.

Statues of Stalin, which once dominated Soviet villages and cities, began to disappear after Khrushchev denounced his former mentor in 1956. De-Stalinization meant the rewriting of history and the renaming of countless streets, factories, dams, and towns. Not even the "hero city" was exempt: in 1956, Stalingrad became Volgograd.

The disorganized condition of the Soviet armed forces at the time of the German invasion had been due to Stalin's earlier purges of senior army officers and party leaders. Khrushchev pointed out that from 1937 to 1941 Stalin had executed many gifted officers at all levels of command. As a result, when Hitler's hordes had commenced hostilities, the Red Army was badly demoralized and poorly led.

Khrushchev also blamed Stalin for the strained relations between the Soviet Union and Yugoslavia. Stalin had broken with Marshal Tito in 1948 because the Yugoslav leader refused to follow Soviet orders. Stalin had then instituted a ruthless purge against so-called Titoites in the other Soviet satellite states of Eastern Europe. Khrushchev said that the Yugoslav leadership had made certain errors but that "these mistakes and shortcomings were magnified in a monstrous manner by Stalin, which resulted in a break in relations with a friendly country."

Khrushchev told his audience that Stalin had said to him, "I will shake my little finger—and there will be no more Tito. He will fall." Khrushchev used this as an example of Stalin's "delusions of grandeur." He added, "No matter how much or how little Stalin shook, not only his little finger, but everything else he could shake, Tito did not fall." Khrushchev had improved relations with Yugoslavia's leadership during his 1955 visit.

Khrushchev also exposed what later became known as the "doctors' plot," in which nine high-level physicians who treated the Kremlin leaders were arrested in Moscow and accused of planning the medical murder of several important government officials. Khrushchev told the party congress that after the arrests, politburo members received copies of the doctors' "confessions of guilt." When the Soviet leaders, familiar with forged evidence, showed their doubt that the confessions were genuine, Khrushchev said that Stalin told them, "You are blind like young kittens; what will happen without me? The country will perish, because you do not know how to recognize enemies." Khrushchev told his audience: "When we examined this [doctors' plot] 'case' after Stalin's death, we found it to be fabricated from beginning to end." That end, suggested Khrushchev, was to set in motion a new, 1930s-style purge in which everybody suspected of disloyalty by Stalin would be swept away.

Khrushchev went on to denounce Lavrenti Beria, Stalin's close associate and head of the secret police. He said Beria had played a key role in the "doctors' plot" and in the arrests, deportations, and deaths of the Stalin years. Beria, who had been executed as "an enemy of the people" soon after Stalin's death, had "stolen into Stalin's confidence," said Khrushchev, by playing on his weaknesses and suspicions.

Yugoslavia's president, Josip Broz Tito (left; 1892–1980), on a stag hunt with Khrushchev in 1956. A World War II hero and a tough and resilient leader, Tito established Yugoslavia's independence from the Soviet Union in 1948. From then on, he tried to steer a neutral course between the Soviets and the West.

Under the bitter stares of Budapest residents, Soviet tanks rumble through the city in December 1956. The Hungarians had fought valiantly for their independence, but they were no match for the 6,000 tanks and tens of thousands of troops sent by Khrushchev. His harsh suppression of the uprising diminished his international prestige.

Finally Khrushchev accused Stalin of creating a "cult of the individual." Worship of Stalin had reached "monstrous size, chiefly because Stalin himself, using all conceivable methods, supported the glorification of his own person." Khrushchev sneered at the "loathsome adulation" in writings about Stalin—even though Khrushchev himself had often written gushing praises of the dictator.

The text of this famous "secret speech" (so called because Khrushchev meant its contents for the ears of the delegates only) was never published in the Soviet Union, but after the U.S. State Department obtained a copy and printed it the following June, a toned-down version was released by the Soviet government. The speech is little known by the Soviet public today. It cannot be found in books, nor is it mentioned at meetings. It is, in fact, one of the many crucial events that have been omitted from official Soviet history.

Still, the speech had a profound impact on communists at home and abroad. Khrushchev's revelations about Stalin's cruel dictatorship created a particular furor in the communist-governed states of Eastern Europe. Some communist leaders in these countries interpreted Khrushchev's speech as a decisive turning away from Stalinism and the beginning of a new era of greater freedom and tolerance. In Poland and East Germany the speech led to public unrest that challenged Moscow's control. But the most dramatic events occurred in Hungary.

In October 1956, after years of discontent under rulers appointed by the Soviets, the Hungarians rebelled openly. In Budapest, the nation's capital, they toppled Stalin's statue. They thought they could achieve independence from Soviet control, as Yugoslavia had managed to do earlier under Tito's leadership.

The people of Hungary rallied around Imre Nagy, himself a communist who had been imprisoned during the Stalin years. Nagy had been premier from 1953 to 1955, but had been removed for criticizing Soviet domination of Hungary. Now the October rebellion brought him back into office.

Khrushchev and the Kremlin leadership were divided over how to deal with the Hungarian uprising. They were uncertain as to which of the two available options—negotiation or armed intervention—would best aid the retention of Soviet control over Hungary. Finally, having gained the support of a group of prominent pro-Soviet Hungarian communists and having secured approval for intervention from other communist states (including China

Their expressions ranging from incredulity to resignation, defendants listen to charges against them during a 1930s "show trial." These trials were highly publicized events in which accusations of treason were "proved" by elaborate false evidence. Probably because of his own involvement, Khrushchev failed to mention the show trials in his 1956 "secret speech."

and Yugoslavia), Khrushchev ordered Soviet armor and mechanized infantry into Hungary to reinforce the Soviet units already stationed there.

On November 4, 1956, Soviet forces in Hungary struck at Budapest and went into action throughout the rest of the country against Hungarian army units and civilian organizations that had remained loyal to Nagy. The Hungarians fought courageously but were no match for the well-equipped Soviet army. After several days of bitter combat, the Soviets succeeded in crushing the revolt.

Within the space of a few months, Khrushchev had swung from his most positive action, the anti-Stalin speech, to his most ruthless decision, the use of Soviet tanks and troops to put down the Hungarian revolution.

Inside the Soviet Union, Khrushchev's denunciation of Stalin upset a number of important officials

Bowing to the inevitable, Premier Bulganin (top right) votes for his own removal in 1958. His title was given to Khrushchev (bottom row, center), who was also named chairman of the Supreme Defense Council. Khrushchev now had complete control of the party, the state, and the military. Bulganin was made head of the Soviet state bank.

who had benefited from their participation in Stalin's terror. Many of them blamed his speech for the unrest in Eastern Europe. These opponents of Khrushchev's policies began plotting to unseat him.

Perhaps the key personality in this behind-the-scenes maneuvering was Mikhail Suslov. An austere and scholarly Marxist theorist, Suslov had survived Stalin's purges by participating in them. He could probably have become a top leader himself, but he preferred to use his skill and influence in a less conspicuous fashion and was essentially satisfied with his position as the party's chief ideologist. Suslov was the total opposite of the outgoing and ebullient Khrushchev, and he must have regarded much of Khrushchev's behavior with disdain.

After the Hungarian uprising, with Suslov on the scene at the Soviet embassy in Budapest, the anti-Khrushchev forces began to come out into the open. Molotov, Malenkov, and Khrushchev's old boss Kaganovich were named to important government posts. These moves were meant to weaken Khrushchev's position as first secretary of the Communist party. Khrushchev fought back by drawing on the grass-roots support he had built up in his extensive travels.

Khrushchev's enemies made their move at a meeting of the party's central committee in December 1956. They agreed to seek to reduce Khrushchev's influence, to bring his most prominent enemies back to power, and to adopt less controversial policies. But Khrushchev outmaneuvered them. In June 1957, at a meeting of the central committee to which his own supporters had traveled from all over the Soviet Union, he decisively reestablished his control over the party and routed his enemies.

All those who had tried to clip Khrushchev's wings were demoted. Molotov was forced to retire. Malenkov was made the director of a factory in a remote province. Others were exiled. By sheer force of personality, and greatly aided by the fact that he had, for several years, taken immense care to build up a solid base of popular support within the party, Khrushchev had turned near-defeat into victory. But he had not heard the last of his enemies.

Mikhail Suslov (1902–1982), one of the Communist party's chief theoreticians, was originally a supporter of Khrushchev, but he was angered by the Soviet leader's denunciation of Stalin. Suslov also disapproved of Khrushchev's break with the Chinese and of his emphasis on the consumer economy at the expense of heavy industry.

7

The Phantom Cows of Riazan

> *We are getting richer, and when a person has more to eat he gets more democratic.*
> —NIKITA KHRUSHCHEV

As the 1950s drew to a close, Khrushchev became increasingly determined to modernize Soviet agriculture, which for years had been woefully outdated and inefficient. He boasted that the Soviet Union would soon produce as much grain, meat, and dairy products as the United States—the most technologically advanced country in the world. To accomplish his ambitious goals, Khrushchev ordered the use of new techniques, tools, and machinery. He reorganized the collective farm system, set up model farms, decreed that vast tracts of previously unexploited territory be turned into farmland, instituted new lifestyles for millions of peasants, and increased the amount of labor that each collectivized farmer was required to perform.

Khrushchev's mixture of impatience and optimism soon proved contagious. All over the country, towns, villages, and entire *oblasts* (administrative regions) were caught up in a production race. Doubters were ignored or ridiculed. Ambitious local leaders traveled to Moscow and pledged increased livestock production.

Experts in the field of animal husbandry (the science of breeding and raising animals) were skepti-

Beaming collective farm workers bask in Comrade Khrushchev's approval of their thriving grain fields. Always a "hands-on" manager, the Soviet leader made frequent visits to the Russian countryside, observing progress and encouraging speeded-up agricultural production.

A Ukrainian peasant family in the 1950s. Khrushchev badly wanted to update Soviet farming methods, but, like Stalin's, his policies were frequently unrealistic. Historian Paul Johnson, a noted critic of Soviet-type social systems, remarked that "No Marxist ever seems to have held sensible views on agriculture, perhaps because neither Marx nor Lenin was interested in it."

cal. Even if cows could somehow be made to give birth to more calves, would there be enough feed for the additional livestock population? Were there enough facilities, grazing grounds, manpower, and equipment to accommodate thousands upon thousands of extra cattle? Were there enough qualified veterinarians and butchers to cope with the projected increases? Would the power stations be able to provide sufficient electricity in response to greater demand from cold-storage plants? One region ignored these and all other questions in a particularly spectacular fashion: the Riazan oblast, which was made up of several agricultural settlements southeast of Moscow. As the Soviet historians Roy and Zhores Medvedev put it in their book *Khrushchev: The Years in Power*, "This hapless oblast was dragged into virtual bankruptcy through the political aspirations of its chief boss." This man, A. N. Larionov, was first secretary of the Riazan oblast committee in 1958, the year in which Khrushchev appealed to oblast committees to increase production in 1959 by a great deal more than the 5% they had managed for the period 1957–58.

Larionov daringly undertook to ensure that his region would double its meat production for the year 1959. To achieve such a huge increase in so short a time is a little like trying to jump over a tall fence from a standing position. Just as a jumper needs a running start to make a successful leap, Larionov ideally would have required a period of preparation, planning, and organization if he was to stand a chance of doubling his region's meat output.

But Larionov did not pause to consider the importance of making preparations. Instead, he called a meeting of local officials and made all kinds of wild claims and promises. His oratory was so effective that by the end of the meeting the Riazan oblast had been committed not just to doubling but to more than *tripling* meat output for the year. In 1958 the region had sold 48,000 tons of meat to the Soviet central meat distribution system; it had now promised to produce and sell a total of 150,000 tons of meat.

The central committee of the Soviet Communist

There were some persons, even scientists in the Soviet Union, who tried to prove that the Dutch have some breed of cows, better cows than our Moscow ones and that our Moscow cows would never be able to compete with them. However, our Soviet cows have derided these scientists and have supported the Central Committee.

—NIKITA KHRUSHCHEV

party was not so confident. At first, the editors of *Pravda* were hesitant to report the aspirations of the Riazan leadership. But Khrushchev insisted that the paper give full coverage to the ambitious plan. Although he had spent much of his life dealing with agriculture, Khrushchev refused to acknowledge that Larionov and his colleagues were being unrealistic. Instead, he encouraged their runaway enthusiasm. Khrushchev saw the pledge as a justification for his own optimistic demands and claims. He even hoped that other regions would follow Riazan's example.

Khrushchev inspects the output of an experimental sheep-raising farm. One of his ideas for increasing Soviet farm output involved replacing the country's small, traditional villages with large, modern communities, to be called agro-towns. The nation's peasants, predictably, opposed the plan.

Oil wells in Baku, an industrial center on the Caspian Sea and a major source of the Soviet Union's petroleum. In 1955 the government began to shift away from the production of consumer goods toward concentration on heavy industry and defense.

Pravda published the Riazan pledge on January 7, 1959. Later that month the Communist party leadership presented its "Seven Year Plan for the Development of the Soviet Union." Pressured by Khrushchev and intimidated by the precedent that had been set in the Riazan, several other regions made similar pledges. Khrushchev quickly made Riazan his pet project. Hardly had the local livestock breeders settled down to try and turn their plan into reality when Khrushchev visited Riazan and gave the region one of the highest awards of the Soviet state, the Order of Lenin.

However, as the Medvedevs point out, "It was clear to even the casual observer that to increase the output of meat and dairy products, or even the number of head of livestock so enormously in one year, was simply out of the question. Nor was it possible to fatten animals enough and thus increase their total weight in so short a time. Since meat purchasing by the state usually began in the fall, it was quite obvious that January was too late a time to start the whole campaign. But excessive publicity and Khrushchev's personal involvement made retreat impossible."

Ultimately, Riazan had to come down out of the clouds and do some very tough arithmetic. The local people had to face facts: In order to deliver three times as much meat, they would either have to triple the number of calves they raised or slaughter many more animals. But every cow killed would mean less milk and fewer calves in the future—a disaster in the long run.

Faced with this difficult situation, the oblast officials decided that one way of beginning to meet their targets without having immediately to deplete the resources of the Riazan collectives would be to commandeer the livestock raised privately by local peasants. The private farmers naturally resented this. Having thus been deprived of their customary sources of milk, meat, and cash, they were then "reimbursed" by the regional officials with nothing but pieces of paper that promised payment at a later date.

As the months went by, Riazan grew desperate in its effort to supply meat in the quantities that its leaders had promised so enthusiastically. Officials were forced to stretch Riazan's resources to the limit. When they ran out of cattle within their own region, they traveled to other oblasts. Trying to keep up the appearance of increasing their own meat production, they bought outside cattle at high prices and then resold the meat to government purchasers for half or less of the original price.

All these transactions and practices were illegal. Officials in other oblasts soon discovered that Ria-

Mechanics study new equipment at a Baku oil refinery. The productivity of Baku and other Soviet industrial centers had long been hampered by red tape and rigid control from Moscow. Khrushchev struggled to reshape the inefficient bureaucratic system and established separate councils to manage the economic affairs of each region.

zan had become a threat to their own attempts at increasing meat output. In their endeavors to stop the escalating depredations of purchasing agents from Riazan, neighboring regions set up roadblocks. The Riazan representatives were often forced to herd cattle from one region to another under cover of darkness.

Gradually, Riazan officials were forced to invent new ways of raising funds to pay for these purchases. They used money originally allocated for machinery and feed. They exhausted credits that should have been spent on housing repair and future building projects. All this was still not enough to fill the unrealistic meat quotas, so they imposed a special tax on the region's residents—payable only in meat! The Medvedev brothers, who lived through this period in the Soviet Union, noted that "these taxes were imposed not only on farms or farmers but were set for all institutions, schools, and even police departments."

"At factories and offices," the Medvedevs said, "money would be collected, designated workers would go to a store and buy the required amount of meat (at 1.5 to 2 rubles a kilo), and then the meat would be brought to a government collection station, where it was sold to the state (at 25 to 30 kopecks a kilo)."

In other words, the people of the region bought the meat at several times the price they received when they sold it to the government. What happened in some other cases was even more absurd. People would, for example, buy butter and then resell it to the government, which then redistributed it to the stores. The cycle would, at times, begin all over again. Because the region got credit for supplying new products every time the government bought recycled goods, it appeared that production was much higher than it actually was. Before long the whole region was stripped of cattle and dairy products, as well as of money and equipment. Many people were deeply in debt.

On December 16, 1959, leaders of the local Communist party addressed an open letter to Khrushchev, whose exhortations had caused all this

It is no secret, after all, that some parents reason thus: 'But my daughter has completed the ten-year course—she cannot possibly milk cows.' She can drink milk, but she considers it beneath her dignity to milk cows.

—NIKITA KHRUSHCHEV
concerning the tendency of Soviet parents to encourage their children to seek white-collar jobs

havoc. The letter claimed that the special drive had been a huge success, and that the region had achieved its aim of tripling meat production to 150,000 tons. Considering that the oblast had used up all its agricultural and financial resources, it seems incredible that Larionov and his colleagues then declared that Riazan would produce between 180,000 and 200,000 tons of meat in 1960.

In their eagerness to help realize Khrushchev's dream of Soviet supremacy in agriculture, the Riazan authorities appeared to have lost touch with reality. The cows that would give the milk or that could be led to slaughter no longer existed. There

In the Ukraine's Riazan district, a newly decorated group of Heroes of Socialist Labor discuss the future of Soviet agriculture with their nation's leader. Khrushchev had given the proud workers their medals for taking part in the Riazan district's ambitious plan to triple its annual meat output.

Residents of Moscow display mixed reactions to a nude sculpture, part of a 1959 art exhibit on loan from the United States. The "cold war" between the West and the Soviet Union thawed somewhat in the late 1950s, when Khrushchev and U.S. President Dwight D. Eisenhower (1890–1969) began to experiment with détente (the relaxation of international tensions).

was clearly no way to fulfill the new pledge. Yet for a few more months the illusion was maintained.

Khrushchev made Larionov a Hero of Socialist Labor and awarded him the Order of Lenin. He praised Larionov's leadership qualities, his tenacity, and his efficiency. School textbooks were revised to describe the "feat" of the Riazan region as an example to be followed by other individuals and work teams.

Before long, however, the entire house of cards collapsed. The livestock was depleted, what little farm equipment remained needed repair, and the work force was impoverished and demoralized. All through 1960 a succession of calamities struck the bewildered populace. Riazan could barely feed itself, much less send vast amounts of meat to the government purchasing centers.

The worst expectations of the more level-headed Moscow specialists came true. Riazan's grain supplies slumped by 50%. Instead of providing up to 200,000 tons of meat, the region could offer only 30,000 tons. An investigative committee came from Moscow and found the region in shambles. On the eve of a Communist party meeting, A. N. Larionov shot himself in his office.

Riazan's dismal plight reflected the state of much of Soviet agriculture in 1960. Meat and grain were in desperately short supply everywhere. Khrushchev, discussing the farm crisis at a January 1961 meeting of the central committee in Moscow, blamed it on poor administration by local officials. He pointed out that party leaders (like the ill-fated Larionov) who bought and resold meat had acted in violation of Soviet law. Khrushchev's optimism, however, did not flag—he continued to require pledges of increased agricultural production—and was ultimately sustained in October 1961, when the Twenty-Second Party Congress unanimously approved his Twenty Year Plan for the nation's future.

A production model of *Sputnik*, history's first artificial earth satellite, on permanent display in Moscow. A source of incalculable pride to the Soviet people, *Sputnik* was launched on October 4, 1957; in the United States the remarkable Soviet accomplishment was greeted by widespread fears and immediate demands that America "catch up" with the Soviet space program.

ATIONAL PRESS CLUB

8

Khrushchev's Visits to the United States

Khrushchev made two trips to the United States. The first, which began on a note of curiosity and suspicion on the part of the American people, ended as a great personal triumph. The second visit was clouded by mutual hostility.

When Khrushchev landed in Washington, D.C., in September 1959, it marked the first visit to the U.S. by a head of the Soviet government and Communist party. The public was interested but wary. Shortly before Khrushchev's arrival, the American people had seen pictures of him in spirited conversation with Richard Nixon (who was then vice-president) at an exhibition of American products in Moscow. The two men had met in a room full of washing machines and other household equipment to conduct what became known as the "kitchen debate," each loudly defending his own country's political and economic system. Many Americans had come to consider the Soviet leader's performance in the debate indicative of a forthright and down-to-earth mentality, a personal quality with which they could identify. At the same time, however, the American public had by no means forgotten the brutal

President Eisenhower and Khrushchev during ceremonies welcoming the Soviet premier to the United States in 1959. Although the two leaders differed on disarmament, West Berlin, and trade relations, they did agree on the importance of ending cold war tensions between their two countries.

Khrushchev addresses the National Press Club in Washington, D.C., in 1959. His reactions to reporters' pointed questions were characteristically blunt and humorous. "If you are going to throw dead rats at me," he told them, "I can throw quite a few dead cats at you."

Reporters and top Soviet officials listen intently as Khrushchev and U.S. Vice-President Richard Nixon (in dark suit; b. 1913) debate at a 1959 exhibition of U.S. products in Moscow. At right is Leonid Brezhnev (1906–1982), Soviet premier from 1977 to 1982.

Soviet suppression of the Hungarian freedom fighters three years earlier, and still associated Khrushchev with the cruel regime of Joseph Stalin.

One event that would overshadow Khrushchev's visit was the completely successful lunar landing made by the Soviet unmanned spacecraft *Lunik II* only a few days prior to Khrushchev's arrival in Washington. This major Soviet achievement surprised and impressed the Americans and gave a certain credence to Khrushchev's claim, "We shall soon be ahead of you on earth as well as out there." To some Americans, Khrushchev's expression of confidence probably seemed even more justified coming as it did not only in the wake of the *Lunik II* mission but also shortly after an American *Vanguard* rocket had exploded on its launching pad, thus providing further evidence that America's own space program was then encountering many problems.

Not knowing quite what to expect of Khrushchev, Americans were surprised and delighted by his smiling, outgoing manner—very unlike the gruff, noncommittal style favored by the two Soviet officials to whom they were most accustomed: foreign ministers Vyacheslav M. Molotov and Andrei A. Gromyko.

At a press conference luncheon in Washington, D.C., Khrushchev stressed the importance of "peaceful coexistence" in the nuclear age and announced that he would address the United Nations on the subject of disarmament during his visit to New York. Many Americans, despite their misgivings about the Soviet leader's Stalinist background, took an optimistic view of Khrushchev's sincerity and good will. Ever the populist, Khrushchev displayed a folksy approach that disarmed both press and public. For a moment, however, he was visited by Stalin's ghost when a reporter shouted "What did you do in the time of Stalin?" The Soviet leader demanded to know who had asked the question. When no one came forward, Khrushchev responded with typical candor: "Well, I did what the questioner has just done. I kept my mouth shut."

The atmosphere that attended Khrushchev's arrival in New York stood in great contrast to the aura of warmth and friendliness that had begun to surround the Soviet leader and his hosts by the time he left Washington. Many of the 25,000 New Yorkers who greeted him at Pennsylvania Station were there because they saw him as a kind of curiosity, and some had come simply to heckle. In what was obviously an attempt to downplay the importance of his visit, Mayor Robert F. Wagner, Jr., neglected to greet Khrushchev personally. However, the Soviet leader remained unperturbed. He managed the crowd civilly and was brought to the Commodore Hotel to lunch with the mayor before checking into his suite at the Waldorf-Astoria. Khrushchev's capacity to face such awkward situations with both equanimity and humor was particularly apparent when, during his visit to New York, the elevator carrying him to his room jammed, leaving the Soviet leader and his entourage stranded between floors for several minutes. Khrushchev simply grinned at his American interpreter and remarked, "Soviet elevators never get stuck."

A major highlight of Khrushchev's first visit to the United States was his speech to the United Nations, in which he made a resounding demand for total disarmament. "In four years," he said, "all the States in the world should be completely disarmed; all armed forces on land, sea, or in the air, should be demobilized; all Ministries of War should be abol-

KHRUSHCHEV:
We must build houses so that they can be lived in by our children and grandchildren.

NIXON:
But our children and grandchildren may have tastes and needs that are different from ours.

KHRUSHCHEV:
Well let them change the furniture. Why change the house.

—quoted from a debate conducted by Khrushchev and Nixon in Moscow in 1959

Visiting Hollywood in September 1959, Khrushchev (in light suit, at center of balcony) enjoys watching actress Shirley MacLaine (center) lead dancers in a scene from the film *Can Can*. The Soviet leader, straight-laced in spite of his bluff manners, was somewhat shocked by the "indecencies" permitted in American movies.

ished; all military bases in foreign countries should be destroyed, military academies closed, and men and material returned for peaceful work in their own countries. Military rockets must be destroyed, and rockets used only as a means of transport and for space flights for the benefit of humanity."

In the course of this speech, Khrushchev also insisted that as "the two biggest countries in the world," the United States and the Soviet Union should develop friendly relations so that "peace on earth will be stable and durable."

Despite the largely positive public reaction that he had encountered in Washington and New York, Khrushchev's reception in Los Angeles was almost frosty. In fact, President Eisenhower became so dismayed by the unenthusiastic welcome that Khrushchev was having to endure that he contacted Norris Poulson, the mayor of Los Angeles, and told him to show Khrushchev proper consideration.

This embarrassing situation was to a great extent saved by the Los Angeles film community. Hollywood's celebrities turned out in force. At a banquet held in honor of the Soviet visitors, Khrushchev's wife, Nina, sat next to Frank Sinatra and charmed everybody with her motherly nature and her considerable command of English. Actress and film star Marilyn Monroe said the gala affair marked "the greatest day in the history of Hollywood." Movie director George Stevens said of Khrushchev, "He is an intellectual. He tries to hide it, but he is."

After a brief stay in San Francisco, during which he met the leaders of several American trade unions, Khrushchev visited Iowa farmer Roswell Garst, whose Coon River acreage was considered a model American farm. In Iowa Khrushchev ate his first hot dog and exclaimed, "We have beaten you to the moon, but you have beaten us in sausage making." It was also in Iowa that Khrushchev gained his first good look at the scale and efficiency of American agriculture, and the quality of the country's farmland. He reacted with a mixture of respect, envy, frustration at Soviet shortcomings, and a new determination to catch up with the United States. Khrushchev was visibly impressed by the bountiful crops he saw while visiting the prosperous Iowa farm and could not help but reflect on the contrast between American farms and the collectives of his homeland. He was amused when Garst chased reporters and photographers away by throwing corncobs at them.

However, not everything American amused Khrushchev during his visit. Unused to public criticism, he reacted angrily to pointed questions asked at the National Press Club in Washington, D.C., and to undiplomatic remarks made by the mayor of Los Angeles. Also, Khrushchev was irritated when he was barred from visiting Disneyland by American secret service officials, who had decided that the appearance there of the controversial Soviet leader would be too risky. More than once, his anger at critics boiled over and he seemed ready to pack up and leave for home.

But he did not. Instead, after a stop in Pittsburgh, he spent two surprisingly relaxed days, September 26 and 27, at Camp David, President Eisenhower's retreat in the beautiful woods of Maryland.

Khrushchev had come to the United States in the shadow of a long-simmering crisis over the status of Berlin. Since the end of World War II, the four victorious powers—the United States, the Soviet Union, Great Britain, and France—had jointly administered the former German capital, which was located deep in Soviet-governed East Germany. The eastern part of Berlin, beyond the landmark Brandenburg Gate, was assigned to East Germany, leaving West Berlin a small enclave of West German territory surrounded by a communist state. The Soviets, who had never liked this situation, wanted exclusive control of the city.

In 1948 the Soviets had tried to starve West Berlin into submission by denying the Western powers road and rail access to the city. For 324 days the Western powers had countered this move by airlifting food, fuel, and other supplies into the beleaguered western sector of Berlin. Stalin and his East German followers had finally become convinced that their tactics had only served to stiffen Berlin's resistance and further alienate public opinion in

It happens that people do not get married for love, but despite that they live their whole lives together. And that is what we want.
—NIKITA KHRUSHCHEV explaining his desire for "peaceful coexistence" with the United States

Khrushchev and American farmer Roswell Garst happily display ears of corn grown on the Iowan's acreage. Ordinarily a staunch booster of all things Soviet, Khrushchev openly admired American farm technology and told Garst his corn was much better than the corn raised in the Soviet Union.

> *Capitalism digs its own grave because it restrains the development of productive forces, gives birth to crises and poverty; because under the capitalist production system the riches are concentrated in the hands of a small group of exploiters, while millions of working people, who create these riches, remain beggars and are deprived of any rights.*
> —NIKITA KHRUSHCHEV
> speaking in February 1959

The Brandenburg Gate marks the border between Soviet-controlled East Berlin and the Western sector of the city. In 1961 East Germany built the Berlin Wall, a massive concrete-block barrier topped with barbed wire and machine-gun emplacements. Its function was to prevent East Berliners from defecting to the West.

Western Europe. But Berlin had continued to be a focus of international tension.

Against this background, the Eisenhower-Khrushchev meeting took on historic dimensions. The year before, Khrushchev had declared that conflict between other countries could be contained, but that "if war breaks out between America and our country, no one will be able to stop it; it will be a catastrophe on a colossal scale." Edward Crankshaw says in his biography of Khrushchev that the concept of peace between the U.S.S.R. and the United States was the Soviet leader's "promise" and that his meeting with Eisenhower was the "seal."

At Camp David, Eisenhower and Khrushchev had a chance to get to know each other. They spoke frankly and simply about their concerns for peace, their private lives, and world affairs in general. Khrushchev publicly expressed his personal liking for Eisenhower. Back in the Soviet Union, he said that he had come to trust the U.S. president and had asked him to pay a return visit. It was decided that Eisenhower would come to the Soviet Union the following spring, and would even bring his grandchildren along.

The two governments agreed, with other major powers, to hold a summit meeting in Paris in May 1960. But a serious crisis intervened. On May 1 of that year, an American U-2 reconnaissance plane was shot down while flying over Soviet territory at

an altitude of 65,000 feet. At first, the U.S. government, presuming that the U-2's pilot had been killed, said the plane had merely been on a flight to gather meteorological data. The Soviets, who up to that point had deliberately not revealed that the plane's pilot was alive, then produced him, and announced that Francis Gary Powers had been carrying papers that proved he was on a spying mission. (U.S. reconnaissance aircraft had, in fact, been violating Soviet airspace for several years, but it was only shortly before the downing of the U-2 that the Soviet Union had finally developed its first antiaircraft missile and thus gained the capability to destroy targets flying at more than 50,000 feet— the maximum altitude then attainable by Soviet fighter planes.)

Washington had no choice but to acknowledge that the U-2 had been conducting a military reconnaissance. Khrushchev, who had committed himself to cooperation with Eisenhower, now found himself sending an official protest to the U.S. government.

Despite this affront to the Soviet Union, and despite the fact that the Americans had not even seen fit to apologize for their actions, Khrushchev said he remained an "incorrigible optimist" and continued to hope that the Paris meeting would be fruitful. When Khrushchev then asked Eisenhower to condemn the previous U-2 flights and to forbid such missions in the future, the president refused. Finally, on May 17, preparations for the Paris summit broke down. Khrushchev called a press conference at which he furiously denounced the United States in general and Eisenhower in particular, accusing both the president and his government of duplicity.

The decision to abandon the Paris meeting came soon after a disastrous encounter between Khrushchev and Moscow's rival for leadership of the world communist movement, Mao Zedong, head of state of the People's Republic of China. This veteran Chinese leader, who had come to power in 1949, regarded himself as senior to Khrushchev and the rest of the Kremlin circle. Their stormy meeting in Beijing led to a withdrawal of Soviet aid to China,

If you want to, go ahead and fight in the jungles of Vietnam. The French fought there for seven years and still had to quit in the end. Perhaps the Americans will be able to stick it out for a little longer, but eventually they will have to quit too.
—NIKITA KHRUSHCHEV
reacting in 1963 to America's increasing involvement in the affairs of Southeast Asia

Francis Gary Powers holds a model of the U-2 spy plane he was flying when he was shot down over the U.S.S.R. in 1960. Convicted on spy charges, Powers was sentenced to 10 years in a Soviet prison, but he was released in 1962 in exchange for a Soviet spy.

THERE'S PLENTY of GARBAGE FLOATING IN THE RIVER TODAY

DEAR K WE ALWAYS WISH FOREIGN DIGNATARIES WELL BUT YOU CAN GO TO HELL

ILA ALL THE WAY HATES MR. K

CRUMMY KHRUSHCHEV GO HOME

CRUMMY KHRUSHCHEV GO HOME

GIVE US OUR FLIERS KEEP OUR FAGS

In sharp contrast to the warm welcome most Americans extended Khrushchev in 1959, these longshoremen greet the Soviet premier in 1960 with an array of hostile messages. The U.S. public was outraged by the Soviets' imprisonment of flyer Francis Gary Powers, and by Khrushchev's torpedoing of the Paris summit conference with President Eisenhower.

including supplies for atomic reactors.

The atmosphere during Khrushchev's second visit to the United States, when he attended a meeting at the United Nations in 1960, was very different from the one that had prevailed during his first. This time there were no smiles, no friendly crowds, no official receptions. As chief of the Soviet delegation to the U.N., Khrushchev was restricted to the borough of Manhattan in New York City, except for weekend visits to Long Island, where the Soviet government maintained a residential estate for its diplomats. Although he had earlier been warmly greeted by Fidel Castro, Khrushchev fumed when the Cuban leader's late arrival for an appointment meant that he was kept waiting outside the Waldorf-Astoria Hotel in front of a battery of whirring television cameras.

It was during the U.N. meeting that Nikita Khrushchev, in sight of the whole world, stepped over the line that separates candor from boorishness. While British Prime Minister Harold Macmillan addressed the General Assembly, Khrushchev banged his fist on the table and shouted at the speaker. Later, Khrushchev demonstrated his disagreement with another speaker by taking off his right shoe, shaking it at the speaker, and then banging it on the desk in front of him. Khrushchev's abandonment of dignity not only shocked many members of the public but also dismayed his colleagues.

The American public always remembered one of Khrushchev's most controversial remarks. When he said to America, "We will bury you," Khrushchev probably meant that communism would ultimately prevail over capitalism and that during this process the Soviet Union would overtake the United States in economic and military power. As a committed socialist and believer in the theories espoused by Marx, Khrushchev was convinced that capitalism contained within itself the seeds of its own destruction and that universal socialism was an inevitability. The remark, however, was misunderstood and taken by the American public as a crude threat to the United States. Regardless, the episode does represent the frustration that characterized Nikita Khrushchev's feelings toward the Soviet Union's major rival.

Khrushchev elicits a smile from Soviet Foreign Minister Andrei Gromyko as he rhythmically pounds his desk at a 1960 session of the United Nations. Khrushchev's fist-pounding and subsequent shoe-banging — traditional Russian gestures of disapproval—astonished the gathered diplomats.

9

Fall from Power

Nikita Khrushchev's eventful rule came to a sudden end in 1964. On October 12 Khrushchev spoke by radio-telephone to three orbiting Soviet cosmonauts and said he was looking forward to meeting them upon their return. The meeting never took place. Khrushchev was toppled from his ruling position three days later. Among those who had agreed that he had to go was his old friend and political ally, Anastas Mikoyan, who stood next to Khrushchev as he was talking to the cosmonauts. Mikoyan had gone to the southern town of Sochi, where Khrushchev was vacationing, to stand by the doomed leader without alerting him to what was in store for him.

The news was communicated to the Soviet people and the world on the evening of October 15. The Soviet news agency, Tass, reported that Khrushchev had been "released" from his duties "at his own request" for reasons of "age and deteriorating health." In actual fact, the leadership group, known then as the presidium of the Communist party, had decided that Khrushchev was a liability. As the years went by, he had grown increasingly erratic, self-centered, boisterous, and unpredictable. He had

Leonid Brezhnev (1906–1982), although one of the prime movers of Khrushchev's downfall, urged that his predecessor be allowed to leave office peacefully. On his "retirement," Khrushchev observed that his most important achievement had been that "they were able to get rid of me simply by voting, whereas Stalin would have had them all arrested."

Khrushchev, drained of his characteristic confidence and high spirits, makes his first public appearance since his October 1964 ouster. A curious but friendly crowd followed the ex-premier and his wife, Nina, as they headed for downtown Moscow to vote in a March 1965 national election.

Mikhail Gorbachev (left; b. 1931), Soviet leader since 1985, and French President François Mitterrand (b. 1916) in Paris in 1985. Mitterrand (who wears headphones carrying a Russian-French translation) and Gorbachev were holding a press conference, the first such event for a Soviet leader in over 20 years.

criticized Stalin for encouraging a "personality cult" about himself, but now the shoe was on the other foot. On October 17 *Pravda* ran a long editorial about the "alien" practice of "the personality cult," an obvious slap at the recently deposed leader.

In the decade of his rule, Khrushchev had made many enemies, including the military leaders who bitterly resented his cutbacks of their funds in favor of expanded investment in agriculture and light industry. Historians now tend to believe that one man was decisive in persuading the Kremlin leadership to abandon Khrushchev: Mikhail Suslov, the Soviet ideologist who had outlasted Stalin's bloody purges, the power scramble among Stalin's successors, and now Khrushchev himself. Suslov, who died in 1982, remained in influential positions throughout the reign of Khrushchev's successor, Leonid I. Brezhnev. At first, Brezhnev governed in partnership with Aleksey N. Kosygin, a rather mild-mannered economist. However, Brezhnev, like Khrushchev, eventually emerged as the single leading personality. He was succeeded, after his death in 1982, by Yuri V. Andropov, who died in 1984. Andropov's successor, Konstantin U. Chernenko, died in 1985. Since Chernenko's death the Soviet Union has been led by Mikhail Gorbachev.

Since its establishment in 1923, the Union of Soviet Socialist Republics has had eight leaders—

Lenin, Stalin, Malenkov, Khrushchev, Brezhnev, Andropov, Chernenko, and now Gorbachev—all of them, to one degree or another, controversial. In order to provide a permanent and unquestioned human symbol of state, the Soviet Union has turned Lenin into a superhuman legend. His idealized image can be found all over the country, in paintings, sculptures, and murals. Virtues are labeled "Leninist" and governing concepts, "Leninism." Often, with a nod backward in history toward Karl Marx, government documents refer to "Marxism-Leninism." The Soviet vocabulary does not, however, contain the word "Khrushchevism."

Most Soviet leaders who leave office under a cloud are simply erased from history books, from monuments, from encyclopedias. They are never mentioned in official statements or speeches. So it was with Nikita Khrushchev, who ceased to exist publicly soon after October 1964.

Khrushchev's downfall was received calmly in the Soviet Union. After being officially denounced for his "hare-brained" schemes and ill-mannered "bragging," he was permitted to live quietly, out of the spotlight.

What was enforced "retirement" like for an energetic, aggressive, and outspoken person like Khrushchev? Here was a man who had been lifted by history to power and prominence, and here, too, was a man who had been unceremoniously hurled from prominence into near-total obscurity.

At first, according to visitors, Khrushchev cut himself off from the world, seemingly not wanting to be reminded of his former existence. He spent most of his time during his final years at his dacha, miles from Moscow. He also maintained a five-room apartment in Moscow, but he rarely visited it. The four-bedroom dacha, built in the 1930s, stood on a seven-acre plot, one of ten such houses in the vicinity.

The Khrushchevs' life in retirement was not lacking in material comforts. Khrushchev's wife did not have to cook or clean. Although the Soviet state calls itself a "classless society," Soviet leaders are usually assigned a large staff of servants. The government

A granite statue of Lenin gazes pensively over Moscow from the Kremlin's formal gardens. This sculpture, erected in 1967, marked a departure from official communist art style, which had traditionally been "heroic"—enormous, idealized, and completely unrealistic.

provided the Khrushchevs with two maids, two cooks, two chauffeurs, a gardener, and, when needed, the services of the same physician who had attended them while Khrushchev was in power.

As he settled into his quiet new way of life, Nikita Khrushchev developed a daily routine. After a simple breakfast, he would go for a long walk with his dog, a German shepherd named Arbat. He often took along a transistor radio, carried in a holster under his left shoulder. The world had known Khrushchev as a heavy, rotund man, but he lost at least 30 pounds during the early months of his retirement. A 1967 report by Jess Gorkin in *Parade* magazine, "What the Russians Have Done to Nikita Khrushchev," described him as leading "a sad and relatively lonely life." Gorkin noted that "Khrushchev sees few people outside his immediate family. Old comrades, including his protégés, avoid him like a plague. It is understandable. After all, they joined forces to oust him from power. Occasionally an old friend will make an appointment to chat, but his many ex-colleagues, even though they live nearby, stay away from this political leper."

Premier Khrushchev congratulates Soviet cosmonauts on April 14, 1961. Like the rest of his countrymen, the Soviet leader was overjoyed by the feat of 27-year-old Yuri Gagarin (right), who, two days earlier, had become the first person in history to orbit the earth.

Also in 1967, the National Broadcasting Company aired a television documentary entitled "Khrushchev in Exile: His Opinions and Revelations," which showed Khrushchev inside and outside his house. The television camera that accompanied him on one of his walks pictured him practicing a new hobby, photography. As analyzed by Jack Gould in *The New York Times*, the camera revealed Khrushchev "as a bent and spent human, his face and posture reflecting the weariness and loneliness of retirement's boredom," and as "one who had achieved the pinnacle of controversial prominence [and] now is the forgotten gardener of his own patch of reminiscences."

At one point, three British reporters happened to find themselves face-to-face with Mrs. Khrushchev at Moscow's Sheremetyevo Airport. She was seeing off a niece who was leaving for Cuba. Nina Khrushchev told the reporters that her husband had been hospitalized twice for a kidney ailment, but that he was "fully recovered and fit and well." She confirmed that he did a great deal of walking and reading. She said that he had just finished the memoirs of General Charles de Gaulle, who was then president of France, and that he "enjoyed them and found them very interesting." Khrushchev had been de Gaulle's guest in France in 1960. "We live quietly these days," Mrs. Khrushchev said. "Our old friends come to see us from time to time, and we have the family, of course."

At that time, the Khrushchev's Moscow apartment was often used by their daughter, Lena, who studied at the Institute of World Economy and International Relations. Another daughter, Rada, was married to Aleksey Adzhubei, who had achieved considerable prominence while Khrushchev was in power. Adzhubei had been fired from his job as editor of the Moscow daily newspaper, *Izvestia*, within hours of Khrushchev's ouster and had been expelled from the Communist party's central committee a few weeks later. The Khrushchevs also had a son, Sergei, as well as Yulia, the daughter of Khrushchev's first marriage. (Yulia's brother, Leonid, had been killed in World War II.)

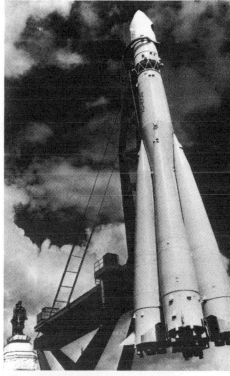

The Soviet spacecraft *Vostok I* is displayed atop a rocket similar to the one that boosted it into space in 1961. After the *Vostok I*'s flight, 7,000 medals—including a third citation as Hero of Socialist Labor to Khrushchev himself—were awarded to those who had contributed "to a new phase in the conquest of space."

An American mother tests her baby's milk for radiation in the early 1960s, when concern about radioactive fallout in dairy products was widespread. Such fears were eased in 1963, when the Soviet Union and the United States agreed to discontinue atmospheric nuclear testing.

The chance encounter at the Moscow airport was unusual. Wives of Soviet officials rarely come into contact with the public, much less with foreign newspaper correspondents. Mrs. Khrushchev's appearances with her husband at voting stations in Moscow were exceptions. On March 12, 1967, some 300 people waited to see the former leader in front of a school on Ryleyev Street. They expected him to arrive by car, but suddenly word spread, "He is coming on foot."

Accompanied by his wife, Khrushchev was walking slowly from his Moscow apartment on Starokonyshny Lane. Henry Kamm, reporting for *The New York Times*, was among the newspeople who had gathered at the voting station. He said the crowd was "eager and excited, but strangely silent." Kamm added: "Few addressed him directly. Those who did said no more than 'Good day, Nikita Sergeyevich,' or 'Long life to you.'" He noted that Khrushchev "smiled in reply, sometimes half-raised his arm in an embarrassed salute and once or twice doffed his large gray hat."

When he was asked whether he was pleased to have so many people greet him, he said, "You know, I worked in Moscow for a long time." Asked if he would like to come out of retirement, Khrushchev replied, "At my age you should not work." He was then 73 years old. During a later encounter at the voting place, on June 13, 1971, he told reporters that he felt well. When asked what he was doing, he

The proper epitaph for Khrushchev's rule remains more impressive than that deserved by many politicians: that he left his country a better place than he found it, both in the eyes of the majority of his own people and of the world.
—MARK FRANKLAND
American historian

answered, "I am a pensioner. What do pensioners do?"

Three months later, Nikita Sergeyevich Khrushchev was dead. On September 12, 1971, the man who had ruled the Soviet Union for a decade died at his country home, at the age of 77, of a heart attack related to hardening of the arteries. His death was not announced for 48 hours, and there was no state funeral. He was buried quietly in Moscow's Novidevichy Cemetery.

Nina Khrushchev died in Moscow on August 8, 1984. Her death went almost entirely unnoticed since the only newspaper to report it referred to her by her maiden name of Kukharchuk and identified her as a "personal pensioner." No reference was made to her husband or to his prominent role in Soviet history.

Khrushchev's successors criticized him severely for paying too much attention to "filling the belly" and not enough to Communist party theory and the

Khrushchev greets U.S. Secretary of State Dean Rusk (b. 1909) at the Kremlin in 1963. Rusk, representing President Kennedy, signed the Nuclear Test Ban Treaty and conferred with the Soviet leader on other ways to reduce East-West tensions.

The Khrushchev family in 1963. From left to right: Galina, wife of the Khrushchevs' son Sergei; Sergei; Nikita and his wife, Nina; Rada, Khrushchev's daughter and wife of Aleksey Adzhubei, editor of the newspaper *Izvestia*; Yelena, Khrushchev's third daughter; and Aleksey Adzhubei.

"economic laws of socialism." Khrushchev must be credited, however, for making serious efforts to improve the living standards of the Soviet people. Although he made some heavy-handed power plays—such as his unsuccessful attempt to install Soviet missiles in Cuba—he tried hard to promote détente, or peaceful coexistence, with noncommunist countries.

The Soviet Union is far from being democratic today, but Khrushchev's denunciation of Stalin paved the way for a less oppressive style of government. It will probably prove to have prevented any possibility of a future return to the brutalities of the Stalin era. In the Soviet Union of the 1980s, Khrushchev remains conspicuously absent from history books, but the mark that he left on his country's history undoubtedly, and deservedly, endures.

Accompanied by her daughters Yelena (right) and Rada (second from right), Nina Khrushchev bids a tearful farewell to her husband on September 13, 1971. Nikita Khrushchev's sparsely attended funeral included a speech by his son. "A man has gone from us," said Sergei Khrushchev, "who had the right to be called a man."

Further Reading

Boffa, Giuseppe. *Inside the Khrushchev Era.* New York: Marzani & Munsell, 1963.

Brown, J. F. *The New Eastern Europe: The Khrushchev Era and After.* New York: Praeger Publishers, 1966.

Crankshaw, Edward. *Khrushchev: A Career.* New York: The Viking Press, Inc., 1966.

Dinerstein, Herbert S. *The Making of a Missile Crisis: October 1962.* Baltimore, Maryland: Johns Hopkins University Press, 1976.

Khrushchev, Nikita. *Khrushchev Remembers.* Boston, Massachusetts: Little, Brown and Company, 1971.

————. *Khrushchev Remembers: The Last Testament.* Boston, Massachusetts: Little, Brown and Company, 1974.

Leonard, Wolfgang. *The Kremlin Since Stalin.* New York: Praeger Publishers, 1962.

Linden, Carl A. *Khrushchev and the Soviet Leadership, 1957–1964.* Baltimore, Maryland: Johns Hopkins University Press, 1966.

McCarley, Martin. *Khrushchev and the Development of Soviet Agriculture: The Virgin Land Program.* New York: Holmes and Meier Publishers, Inc., 1976.

Medvedev, Roy A. and Zhores A. Medvedev. *Khrushchev: The Years in Power.* New York: Columbia University Press, 1976.

Pistrak, Lazar. *The Great Tactician: Khrushchev's Rise to Power.* New York: Praeger Publishers, 1961.

Rush, Myron, *The Rise of Khrushchev.* Washington, D.C.: Public Affairs Press, 1957.

Tatu, Michel. *Power in the Kremlin: From Khrushchev to Kosygin.* New York: The Viking Press, Inc., 1969.

Wolfe, Bertram D. *Khrushchev and Stalin's Ghost.* New York: Praeger Publishers, 1957.

Chronology

April 17, 1894	Born Nikita Khrushchev, in Kalinovka, Russia
Oct. 1917	Bolsheviks seize power from Provisional Government in second stage of Russian Revolution and establish communist rule
1918	Khrushchev joins Bolshevik party and enlists in Red Army
April 1922	Joseph Stalin appointed general secretary of Russian Communist party
Jan. 21, 1924	Vladimir Lenin dies
1925	Khrushchev appointed party secretary for Yuzovka region
1926–27	Stalin ousts rivals from party leadership and consolidates position as dictator
1929	Khrushchev appointed chief of party cell at Industrial Academy in Moscow
Dec. 1, 1934	Assassination of Leningrad party chief, Sergei Kirov, prompts Stalin to initiate mass purge of Communist party
1935	Khrushchev elected first secretary of Moscow region party committee
1938	Appointed first secretary of Ukraine
1939	Appointed to party's political bureau
June 22, 1941	Germany invades Soviet Union
May 2, 1945	Soviet forces take Berlin
March 5, 1953	Stalin dies
	Georgi M. Malenkov named first secretary of Communist party of Soviet Union
March 15, 1953	Khrushchev replaces Malenkov as first secretary
Feb. 1954	Launches Virgin Lands program, a massive project intended to increase Soviet grain output
July 1955	Attends summit meeting in Geneva with representatives of major Western powers
Feb. 24, 1956	Denounces Stalin in speech to Twentieth Party Congress
Nov. 4, 1956	Orders Red Army into Hungary to crush anti-Soviet uprising
Jan. 1958	Appointed prime minister
Sept. 1959	Visits the United States for talks with President Dwight D. Eisenhower
Oct. 16, 1962	John F. Kennedy, president of the United States, learns of Soviet deployment of nuclear missiles on the Caribbean island of Cuba
Oct. 22, 1962	Kennedy announces security crisis, demands withdrawal of Soviet missiles, and imposes naval blockade of Cuba
Oct. 28, 1962	Khrushchev agrees to dismantle missile sites on condition that U.S. government ends blockade and promises not to invade Cuba
Oct. 15, 1964	Ousted as first secretary by rivals in party leadership
Sept. 12, 1971	Dies, aged 77, at country home outside Moscow, of a heart attack

Index

Martin Ebon served with the Office of War Information during World War II, and later with the Foreign Policy Association and the U.S. Information Agency. Among his more than sixty books are the encyclopedic *World Communism Today* and the biographies *Malenkov: Stalin's Successor, Svetlana: The Story of Stalin's Daughter, Che: The Making of a Legend,* and *Lin Piao: the Chinese Communist Leader.*

Arthur M. Schlesinger, jr., taught history at Harvard for many years and is currently Albert Schweitzer Professor of the Humanities at City University of New York. He is the author of numerous highly praised works in American history and has twice been awarded the Pulitzer Prize. He served in the White House as special assistant to presidents Kennedy and Johnson.